1

A FORK IN THE CART PATH

**a struggling bogey golfer
considers giving up the game forever**

Randy Stewart

*in honor of
every bogey golfer*

CONTENTS

FOREWORD

What an honor and privilege it was for me to be a part of Dr. Stewart's journey from July 2014 to July 2015! I have known him since my childhood, when my family moved to Arab, Alabama. I was fortunate to have been included in several Christmas dramas written and directed by him during his years of ministry at Arab First Baptist Church. From my high school days to the present, he has always been an inspirational role model for me and my family. My two daughters refer to him as "Uncle Randy". We are better people for having him and his family in our lives.

I spent over ten years promoting and teaching the great game of golf as a club professional. I prided myself in being a student of the game, striving to learn every aspect from the tee to the green. I was extremely interested in helping others play the game, so I also became a student of golf instruction. I quickly discovered that not every student takes away the same thing from a lesson experience with a particular teacher, that *how* I communicate is as important as *what* I communicate. I often found myself wondering if a thought or process that was effective for me would register with my students during a lesson.

Fortunately, I had the opportunity to read a book by Michael Hebron called *Golf Swing Secrets and Lies: Six Timeless Lessons*. It included many photographs of great golfers from the early 1900s to the present day. Hebron's main point of emphasis was the striking similarity in how the game has been played from a technical swing perspective. Then and now, all good golfers put their club in virtually identical positions during the swing to achieve maximum control of the ball at impact. Using this knowledge, I began to wonder what would happen if I tried to communicate these universal concepts to my students. What if I taught them the things that *must* happen during a golf swing, the *key swing habits* of every great golfer? Would this improve their ability to learn to play better golf? The answer, I discovered, was an emphatic "yes!"

Today I am no longer a club professional. In fact, I refer to myself as a letter-carrying amateur. I decided to pursue other ventures than golf, so I applied to the USGA for reinstatement of my amateur status. Once that request was granted, my days as a golf instructor came to an end. The desire to play and teach, however, has never left me. I am now able to play a few amateur events each year and hope to find time to enjoy the game more often. But, until recently, teaching golf has not been on my agenda.

With the itch to teach still present, I found Dr. Stewart's invitation to be his instructor too good to turn down. We both looked at this as a chance to complete some unfinished business. Years earlier, while I was still teaching the game professionally, we played together during a round at our local public course. Dr. Stewart, a habitual slicer of the ball, wanted to learn to hit a shot that curved in the opposite direction, right to left. In golfing terms, he wanted to hit a draw. I spent some time with him after that round and gave him a simple thought to help him accomplish his goal. By the time we went home, I had transformed him into a "drawing" monster. Unfortunately, that was the only interaction we had as

10

student and teacher. I went back to Georgia, where I lived at the time, with a promise to continue our lessons if the opportunity arose in the future. When we moved back to Arab a few years ago, that opportunity materialized. That's why, when I received his email last June telling me about the "massacre" he had experienced and asking me to be his golf instructor, I was more than eager to complete the work we had begun.

Since that day, I have been flattered and honored to be the one chosen to help my friend on his journey. He has done his part as a student, maintaining his focus and commitment. A particularly commendable quality has been his ability to manage his time to allow for ample practice and adequate thought before and after each lesson. This is a skill all too often overlooked by people wanting to improve their golf games. From the day we began our journey on the putting green to the day we ended it on the same putting green, he has been a faithful pupil. The time in between, for sure, has not always been easy for him. As you will read, his confidence has risen and fallen many times over the course of our time together, typical of all who try to improve their games. He has often compared himself to the Israelites wandering in the desert, searching in vain for the Promised Land.

I am happy to report that, like the Hebrews, Dr. Stewart's wilderness experience lasted only for a time. He has found golf's Promised Land, although much later than he anticipated and by a different route than he imagined. The game of golf tends to parallel life, and his journey has been no exception. It has tested his honor, respect, self-reliance, mental toughness, and decision-making. It has forced him to deal with the pressure that comes with both success and failure. As you read this book, you will see frustration, triumph, joy, despair, defeat, and thankfully victory. You will also hear a wonderful testimony about something else this great game provides to each of us who play it... hope!

Dr. Stewart sent me this manuscript chapter by chapter during our time together as pupil and teacher. As I read the rough drafts along the way, I found myself wishing the next lesson would come so I could get an email with another chapter. I predict that you will likewise move quickly from one chapter to the next. He offers you an honest, humorous, and heartwarming account of the events that transpired over those fifty-two weeks.

Thank you, Dr. Stewart, for the front-row seat over the past year! I enjoyed every moment we spent together. I look forward to seeing you on the golf course soon.

Jonathan Lynch

Chapter 1: Drawing a Line in the Sand Trap

I am fifty-eight years old and am facing an unexpected life choice, an unforeseen fork in the path ahead. As I type these words, I am seriously considering giving up the game of golf... forever.

The decision before me is not fueled by emotion. It has nothing to do with time pressure or health issues. It doesn't stem from boredom with or mastery of the game. As you will soon discover, I have not fine-tuned my swing, accomplished all my golfing goals, and thus lost all motivation to play. Just the opposite is true. I am contemplating retirement from golf because my game is so horrendous I no longer enjoy playing.

My love affair with golf began as a teenager. I have played the game poorly for over four decades. I can boast of a few personal highlights, the details of which I will share in subsequent chapters, but can also lament a plethora of lows which are the focus of this book. I still adore most aspects of this alluring game: its aesthetic beauty and rich heritage, its applicability to everyday life, its challenge and its charm. Nevertheless, there is one aspect of golf—my own game—that I no longer love and, in fact, have come to loathe. My lack of golfing skills has become an ever-present thorn in my golf shoe, a cross I must constantly bear from tee to green. I am no longer willing to carry the weight of that cross, to feel the painful prick of that thorn.

"Increasingly embarrassing" are two words that best describe my feelings about my golf game. Although I like to refer to myself as a bogey golfer, the truth is actually worse. Bogey golf is my goal at the start of each round, but 90% of the time I fall short of that mark. On rare occasions my score will dip into the high 80s, but just as often it will soar into triple digits.

As you probably could guess, my plus-100 days have become more frequent in recent weeks. During this slump, I have tried to lower my expectations by starting a few rounds with double-bogey golf as my goal but, sad to say, have likewise failed. Fortunately, most of this atrocious scoring has come when I have played alone, but a few dismal performances have been in full view of family or golfing peers, all of whom seem amazed at the self-inflicted wounds I incur from hole to hole. Instead of instant shouts of praise—"Great shot!" or "Looks good!"—my swings are all too often followed by an uncomfortable silence and the shaking or lowering of heads. When I hear compliments from my partners, it's usually because I have finally reached the green, even if my ball is still fifty feet from the cup.

One way or the other, the days of such lousy golf by Randy Stewart are coming to an end. As Roberto Duran once said to Sugar Ray Leonard, "No mas!" I have drawn a line in the sand trap. No longer will I always be the worst golfer in the foursome. Gone are the days of personal golfing futility and embarrassment. I have served golf the divorce papers and, unless things change for the better, will soon sign them and leave the game behind.

In the meantime, there still remains an opportunity for reconciliation, but only if golf meets my terms: improvement. As I alluded to earlier, I see myself riding down a cart path with a fork looming ahead. To the right is the path of *more golf*, to the left the path of *no golf*. What happens in the next few weeks will determine which direction I head. If my game improves, I will choose *more golf*. If there is no improvement or, heaven forbid, a further decline, then golfing for me will be history. Unless my game becomes bearable, I will treat golf like I do football and basketball, as sports I once played. I will watch golf on TV as a spectator instead of a fellow gladiator. As for my clubs, I will give them to relatives or sell them on eBay. If a set of clubs yields only a specific number of great golf shots, and no more, the person who inherits mine should have many good rounds ahead.

As you can tell by my remarks above, I have not yet thrown in the golfing towel. The upcoming fork in the cart path is still a considerable distance away. Maybe, just maybe, I will get better as I approach it. Perhaps I will be able to salvage my game and continue my once-favorite pastime.

I understand what's at stake. My sincere desire is to play golf for many years to come. I will be disappointed if I have to lay down my clubs. I will not miss my own game, but I will sorely miss the game itself. Because of this, I have developed a one-year plan of action that will make success more likely. My plan has three interlocking parts: instruction, practice, and reporting. In short, I will seek the instruction of a trusted teacher, practice what he preaches, and report my progress along the way. My friend, Jonathan Lynch, a former club professional, will be my teacher. The driving range, putting green, golf course, and the five inches between my ears will be my practice facilities. A weekly narrative, written by me, will be my recording method, essentially an autobiography of my progress, or lack thereof.

The book you hold in your hand is that diary. I am inviting you to join me over the next year as I walk toward that fork in the cart path. Misery loves company, it is often said, but so does success. Whatever the outcome, good or bad, I will greatly appreciate your presence along the way. As you read these pages, you will become part of a gallery watching this troubled hacker determine his golfing future. My hope and prayer is that your head will not look down too often in embarrassment or turn away in disgust, that I will actually begin to hear you shout "Great shot!" before I start to putt. One warning, however, is necessary. Until my game improves, I advise you to walk behind me. Anyone standing in front, even to my side, is in much peril.

Yesterday I started the first week of my plan, and I will give you my initial report at week's end. In the meantime, I think it would be helpful to share with you more of my golfing history, my personal pilgrimage from previous mediocrity to present mayhem. This will be the subject of the next four chapters.

Chapter 2: A Poor Foundation

Like so many golfers, I was introduced to the game by my father. A Southern Baptist minister, he started playing during his seminary days in Kentucky when he and two other young preachers, Harlice Keown and Arnold Porter, would drop their studies and head to a Louisville course. This threesome remained friends for life, the golf course and their churches becoming favorite places of rendezvous. One of my fondest golfing memories is occasionally joining them as a fourth partner, observing firsthand their love for the game and for each other. That Dad was the worst golfer of the three didn't seem to bother him. Something greater than golf was being played every time they met, and he knew it. Eventually, he did outscore his buddies in one key area. Now eighty-eighty years old, he is the lone survivor of the three.

From the first time he swung a driver at the age of thirty to his last competitive putt in his eighties, my father was a below-average golfer. With few exceptions, my golfing history has tended to mirror his, lending credence to the adage that an acorn doesn't fall far from the tree. Like me, he never improved much during his life. Like me, his game took a nosedive as he approached sixty, becoming less and less enjoyable to play. The low point for him came a few years ago when my wife, Cathy, and my brother's wife, Sarah, both casual golfers, shot lower than him during a family outing. He has never played another round since. Faced then with a similar decision as

I face now, he took the *no golf* fork that day. He retired a defeated golfer.

This man, my first hero in life, was also my first instructor in golf. I remember him taking me to the nearest public course, handing me a club, showing me how to grip it and swing it, then watching my first futile attempts at contact. I remember his words of instruction and correction as I was trying to learn the game. I recall how much better he was compared to me and that my first golfing goal was to beat him on just one hole. He had a love for the game that was contagious, and I am so thankful he passed that love to me.

There was one problem with this arrangement, however, a problem that set me straight on a path to golfing mediocrity. As you have probably guessed, I was being taught the fundamentals of golf by someone who had little knowledge of golf fundamentals himself. As far as I know, my dad never had a golfing lesson, never went to a range between rounds, and never purchased golf instructional manuals or books. He had little, if any, awareness of the basics of golf necessary to play well. When he introduced me to the game, he introduced me to *his* game. Almost everything about my swing—the grip, setup, takeaway, downswing, and follow-through—I learned from him and have never unlearned. If it is true that the first instruction of a golfer's career is the most important, it was almost a certainty my game would turn out the way it did.

In no way am I trying to cast my father in a bad light. I wrote above that he is my hero, and I meant it. His father, Thurston Stewart, died of tuberculosis at the young age of twenty-seven, leaving behind a wife,

Pauline, with three children under the age of six and an unborn child in her womb. Never remarrying and never learning to drive, my grandmother raised those four children by selling Avon products door to door. My dad, eighteen months old when his father died, never experienced what it was like to go fishing or golfing with his dad. But he was the best father I could ever have hoped for. He once told me he learned how to be a father by staying close to his heavenly Father. I believe him. I could go on and on about his incredible life—his service in the Army near the end of World War II, his sixty-six year marriage to my second hero, his fifty-year ministry to Christ in Kentucky and Tennessee, his successful fight against laryngeal cancer in his fifties. He is the greatest man I have ever met, and there are no close seconds. Although he may not have known the fundamentals of golf, he knew the fundamentals of life, and I am grateful beyond words that he helped me get a grip on them.

Besides the greatness of his life off the course, there are two other reasons I harbor no ill feelings toward him for my personal golfing woes. For one thing, he didn't have much of an opportunity to improve his own game. He had the time constraints of a being a pastor, the inconvenience of living thirty minutes from the nearest public course, a limited financial reserve that made "buying a game" impossible, and a lifelong commitment to place family before golf. If his situation had been different and he had sought proper instruction, I am confident that his golf game would have improved. I also have no doubt that he would have then passed those good basics on to me as eagerly as he did the bad ones years before. In a sense, he never had the chance to help me like he wanted to help me.

This leads straight to the final reason that I have to take it easy on my dad. Unlike him, I have had every opportunity to improve my game. I have lived adjacent to a fairway or in a golfing community for over twenty years. I pass by a driving range every day as I go to and from my home. What's more, my income as a physician has given me the flexibility to afford golfing lessons. Unfortunately, I have chosen otherwise. It is true that my schedule is demanding and that my family and faith come first, but it is also true that I could have made time for proper golf instruction if I had really wanted it. If I find myself today in dire golfing straits, it is wrong for me to lay the blame on what my father did or did not relay to me years ago. There has been ample time and opportunity since then to right the ship. To see who is ultimately to blame, someone needs to hand me a mirror.

In summary, my golfing career got off to a rocky start because of a poor foundation taught to me by my father and because of my unwillingness thereafter to make the sacrifices necessary to build a newer and stronger foundation. The result has been four decades of horrible golf, poorly played and often humorous, some details of which I will share in the next chapter.

Chapter 3: Swing Thoughts of a Bad Golfer

If a homebuilder pours a weak foundation and places a flimsy structure on top of it, the result is a house that will collapse during a storm. This is analogous to my golf game. My dad laid a poor foundation. Upon it, I built an equally poor structure. I should have been smart enough to know where this would lead. It was almost a guarantee that my golf game would not be able to weather the storms it faced during a round. I was in the same position as those two little pigs living in houses of straw and sticks. Everything seemed fine until the Big Bad Wolf of Golf paid me a visit. My game would then crumble. One huff and puff was all it would take.

It is hard for good golfers, safely residing in houses of stone, to understand the plight of people like me in shaky golf dwellings. They may sympathize with us, but true empathy—walking in our spiked shoes—is unlikely. Consequently, the best person to explain the psyche of a bad golfer is someone like me, a bad golfer himself. This requires either raw courage or blind stupidity on the part of the storyteller, who must openly confess a litany of personal golfing failures. It's not a pleasant task at any time but is especially painful when good golfers are in the audience. Think again of those two little pigs. When they crawl out of the rubble that was once their houses, the last porky they want to meet is that smart pig, the one whose house is still intact. What's more, the last thing they want to do is field questions from him about their experience. "How did you feel as your house fell down?

What did you do to try to save yourself? Did it hurt? Was it hard to breathe under there? Didn't you know that your house was substandard?" In the same way, it is hard for a wee little golfer like me to answer questions like these without becoming red-faced in embarrassment or anger.

I have played hundreds of rounds of golf in my life and all too often have found myself lying beneath the rubble of the flimsy game I built around me. In this chapter, I want to crawl out of the debris and tell my story. I want to share what it's like to be an aspiring bogey golfer, to relate how the mind of an occasional triple-digit scorer works during a round. I'll let you decide whether it's brave or foolish for me to do so.

Perhaps the best way I can help you understand my psyche is to share twelve common thoughts that go through my mind during a typical day of golfing chaos. Ironically, I will do so in orderly fashion. I will begin at the first tee as I reach into my golf bag for a ball and will end at the eighteenth green as I remove my cap and give my playing partners a congratulatory handshake.

1. "Any golf ball will do."

Many golfers prefer to play with a particular ball. They claim their favorite brand travels farther or spins better. Although I believe them, I cannot relate to what they are saying. My game has not evolved enough to feel a difference between one ball and another. I have three criteria for using a golf ball: it must be hard, round, and have dimples. I don't care what color it is, how compressible it is (whatever this means), what corporate logo it bears, if it is marketed for women, or if it has X-OUT stamped around its equator. I have discovered that my problem is not the brand of ball but how my clubface hits it. Any golf ball, no matter how expensive, goes dead right when shanked, into the water when hit fat, over the green and into the woods when hit thin. That's why my bag is filled with an assortment of balls. My picky friends know this and will give me any off-brand they happen to find. I accept each ball gladly, aware that I will probably lose it again later in the round.

2. "I must feel my way around the course."

Some golfers are technical players. They focus before every swing on proper technique. Others are feel players, relying more on instinct with each shot. Since I have virtually no technique, I am a feel player by default. There is, however, an inherent problem with feel-only golf. Trying to feel a golf swing during a whole round is the same as trying to feel in love during a whole marriage. It's just not possible. Sooner or later, the feeling wanes and the harder work—technique in golf, commitment in marriage—must take center stage. Since I have no technical golf knowledge, I have nothing to fall back on when the feeling departs. And that's usually when things get very ugly for me.

3. "Play fast!"

Everyone comments on my speed of play. Before you can say *double bogey*, I address the ball and put it into flight. I play fast for two reasons. For one thing, nobody likes to play behind or alongside a slow golfer, especially when that slowpoke strikes the ball a hundred times a round. The faster I play, the more enjoyable it is for those around me. I am merely being considerate. The other reason I play at such a rapid pace has to do with being a feel player. To rely totally on instinct, I try to swing the club with a clear head, not entertaining any thoughts about how to swing. Instincts work better without such clutter. For this reason, I play my shots quickly, before my mind has the opportunity to engage.

4. "I hit my woods better than my irons."

My driver is the most reliable club in my bag. I'm not very long, but I'm fairly straight and usually in the fairway off the tee. I am consistent as well with my other woods. The story is much different with irons. I hit all irons, conventional or hybrid, with the predictability of the stock market. The greater the loft, the more unsure the result. Therefore, given the choice between a wood and an iron, I will always reach for the former. Most good golfers, in contrast, would choose the latter. My set of fourteen clubs—which includes 1, 3, 5, 7, 9, and 11 woods—seems strange to good golfers. So does my game.

5. "I play worse as I get closer to the hole."

Most good golfers salivate when faced with an approach less than a hundred yards from the pin. They are confident they can dial that number into their wedges and execute the shot with precision. If I were to hit a few balls from the same place in the fairway, the results would be woefully different, enough to make a young child wince. There are many reasons my short game is so bad. Too little practice, improper technique, and a tendency to choke under pressure are the first three that come to mind. It is also important to remember that I prefer a wood to an iron and that there is no wood I can pull out of my bag when I'm less than one hundred yards from the flag. Given the choice, I would rather have a 7-wood in my hand from 160 yards away than a 9-iron at the hundred-yard marker. I suspect this will have to change during the next year if my game is to improve.

6. "I need to change my swing... now."

Believe it or not, I have four different swings at my disposal during a round of golf. With swing #1, I take the clubhead straight back along the line of flight then swing straight through. During swing #2, my club approaches the ball from the outside, favoring a fade (or slice). Swing #3 is just the opposite, an inside-to-outside downswing and a tendency to draw (or hook). I alternate these three swings, often during the same round, based on the way I am playing and how I feel. When all else fails, I resort to Swing #4, which is essentially a very short backswing and follow-through, similar to that seen with pitching. With this, I hit the ball low and straight but also very short. How short? My 5-iron shot travels a grand total of one hundred yards when struck this way. I suspect good golfers who read this will either arch their back in laughter or bend at the waist to vomit. Even bad golfers should be amused or nauseated at my tendency to bounce from swing to swing as I go from hole to hole. If not, let me give them a warning. Please, please do not try this. It is the golfing equivalent of Multiple Personality Disorder and is equally deserving of psychiatric care.

7. "People tend to play well when I'm around."

Want to have the round of your life? Then play with me. Want to hit a shot you will always remember? Ask me to join your foursome. For whatever reason, my presence brings out the best in my playing partners. Why is this so? I think it has something to do with me being such a bad golfer. Most golfers are proud and competitive by nature and have a strong desire to impress the others playing along with them. Deep inside, they are afraid their game will not measure up to those in the group. Playing with me, such fears are erased in a couple of holes. In fact, the opposite emotion—the relaxed enjoyment of superiority—takes over. In this frame of mind, they are free to play some of the best golf of their lives.

8. "I appreciate that piece of advice."

By and large, golfers are a benevolent group of people, ready and willing to help those less fortunate than themselves. When they see me on the golf course or practice tee and realize how needy I am, they quickly come to my rescue. Over the past forty years, well-meaning golfers have bestowed on me hundreds, if not thousands, of golfing tips. These pointers have come in various times, places, and forms. Some have been given to me during a round, some after the round is over, a few (from those who have played with me previously) before the round starts. I have received swing advice in the hospital dictation room (from a fellow physician who thought he had diagnosed me), in the church sanctuary on Sunday (from a friend who played with me on Saturday), in the clubhouse bathroom (from a playing partner standing at an adjacent urinal), and on a subway in New York City (from a stranger who overheard me lament my golfing woes). These helpful hints are most often presented in face-to-face dialogue, but sometimes they have been sent to me via phone call, email, or text message. That I have not received advice on Facebook or

Twitter can be explained by the fact that I have never had a Facebook page or Twitter account. Occasionally, a friend will walk up to me and place an entire instructional book in my hand, urging me to read it. For what it's worth, a book is perhaps the most humiliating way to give advice to bad golfers like me. It signifies to us that our flaws are too great to be addressed in a single text, email, or conversation. It's similar to what a Catholic gentleman at confession would feel if the priest, instead of offering immediate forgiveness, handed him the entire Bible.

9. "A sand trap is my worst nightmare."

Of all of golf's many hazards, the greenside bunker is my Achilles heel. Instinct and feel seem to vanish the second my feet touch the sand and with them any hope of a respectable score. I am actually pretty adept at getting out of fairway bunkers, because I have no trouble hitting the ball before the sand. Just the opposite is true, however, around the green. I have yet to master the feel of striking the sand instead of the ball. My percentage of successful sand exits in one swing is less than fifty. If the lie is a "fried egg", on a downslope, or up against the lip, the odds diminish exponentially. General Custer had a better chance getting out of his dilemma.

10. "Bogey putts fall. Par putts fail."

My tendency to wilt under pressure during a round of golf defies explanation. It's not that I am immune to acting under pressure in other areas of my life, and it can't be blamed on fear of performing in front of a crowd. As an emergency room physician for eighteen years, I faced pressure situations every day far greater than a golf shot and handled them with calmness and precision. I have served as a music minister for twenty-five years and have felt at ease with a thousand eyes watching my every move. Why, then, does a four-foot putt for par in front of three of my friends set my nerves on fire? Furthermore, why is this nervous tension absent when I have the same putt for bogey? These are unanswerable questions. You might as well ask God why we have an appendix. My only recourse is to try to deal with it, and this I have done. Since I should be in the Bogey Putt Hall of Fame, I have tried to imagine that my par putt is for bogey. This hasn't worked. Nor has it helped to pretend I'm putting in the trauma room or the sanctuary. My inner golfing demons are not fooled so easily. Like so many other aspects of my game, I don't have a solution. My only hope is that Jonathan, my golf instructor, is also an exorcist.

11. "Perhaps the law of averages will come into effect on my next shot."

A blind squirrel, if persistent, will stumble upon an acorn. A basketball novice, given enough chances, will throw a ball through the hoop from center court. Likewise, a bad golfer, given a hundred swings, is bound to hit at least one pure shot during a round. If he plays forty years, like I have, the law of averages guarantees that every now and then he will accomplish the incredible.

I know the percentages all too well. A big reason I continue to play is the experience of hitting a great shot out of nowhere. The satisfaction associated with it ranks up there with the joy of seeing your child born or your lottery number displayed. I remember playing in a four-man scramble a few years ago at a local charity event. No thanks to me, my team was only one stroke back with two holes to play. I was swinging so poorly that we had not used my ball once to that point. On the seventeenth and eighteenth holes, however, the law of averages raised its head as I sank two winding birdie putts, each greater than forty feet in length, securing for my team the first place prize. The thrill of that bizarre success remains palpable today.

By far, the two most incredible golf shots in my life have occurred on the par-three eighth hole at my home course. During April six years ago, I was playing alone, my wife riding along as a spectator. The pin placement was toward the back edge, leaving a 165-yard shot from the blue tees. With a strong wind behind me, I took my 9-wood out of the bag and launched the ball straight on line with the flag. I remember saying, "That looks good!" while it was in mid-flight. When the ball disappeared from sight, I assumed it had rolled off the back of the green. I was wrong. It was a hole-in-one!

Expecting to wake up at any moment, I floated down the ninth fairway and into the clubhouse to collect the money that had accumulated in the hole-in-one pot. The response was not what I expected. The golf pro apologetically informed me that my ace did not qualify because it had been witnessed only by my wife. Seeing my shoulders slump and my look of disappointment, he retreated to the business office to confer with accounting. A few minutes later, he returned with a compromise. I was to be awarded the money in the pot, but my hole-in-one was not to be acknowledged on the plaque that hangs in the grille area. And that's exactly what happened. If you go to the clubhouse today and read the names of golfers who have had holes-in-one, you will not see my name included. Such is the lot of a bad golfer. I blame my wife. Apparently, she cannot be trusted.

Two years later—playing during the same month, on the same hole, with the same pin placement, but without my wife as a witness—I watched my 5-wood shot land in the center of the green, scoot forward twenty feet, and dive into the hole like a groundhog. I jumped up and down in glee and then, like the young boy in the television commercial, looked in every direction to see if anyone by chance had been watching. When I realized that no eyewitnesses existed, I proceeded to Plan B. I got in my cart, drove to the adjacent ninth tee, and interrupted a player in mid-swing. He happened to be one of our local family physicians. "Bo," I said excitedly, "I have not gotten out of my cart since I left the eighth tee. Would you go pick my ball out of the hole?" After a high five from all the members of the group, my fellow doctor walked to the eighth green, lifted the Callaway from the cup, and threw that mounted-and-never-to-be-hit-again ball back to me. Once again, I floated down the ninth fairway. Recalling my experience two years earlier, I knew better than to share my hole-in-one with the clubhouse pro.

A few years earlier, I witnessed a hole-in-one as a playing partner. I was with Earnest McGee and his two sons, Michael and Dusty, at Twin Lakes Golf Course. Its eighth hole was a par four which had been shortened to par-three length because the longer tees were closed for repair. After I hit my drive, I watched Dusty use a fairway wood to propel his ball onto the green and into the hole. After the round, the four of us told the golf pro about Dusty's feat. No hole-in-one pot existed to tap into, but the pro made sure the ace was acknowledged in the local newspaper, along with the names of Dusty's playing partners. Several people who read the article joked with me, saying, "Dusty better be glad you were playing with him. I wouldn't believe any claim of a hole-in-one by three McGees!" By the way, that's eerily similar to what the golf pro insinuated about my wife and me after my first ace. The only difference is that he wasn't kidding.

Last year I was in earshot of another hole-in-one. I was teeing off on the par-five sixth hole at my home course when I heard triumphant shouts from the eighth tee not far away. (Yes, the same eighth hole, the site of my two aces.) I looked in that direction and saw three golfers high-fiving a fourth, patting him on the back. I knew immediately what had happened, walked over to their tee, and offered my congratulations.

If you are keeping score, in my lifetime of golf I have hit two holes-in-one, witnessed one hole-in-one, and heard yet another hole-in-one. Both of mine have an asterisk by them. None of the others do. Such is my luck, the lot of a bad golfer. In all honesty, the lack of eye-witnesses to my aces doesn't bother me very much. God knows what happened those two April days on the eighth hole of Cherokee Ridge Golf Course. Anyone who has doubts needs to take it up with Him. I'm just thankful that it happened to me, the unlikeliest of candidates. Now, having experienced such golfing grace, I always step to the first tee wondering if something like this could happen to me again. The law of averages quickly answers back: "Yes, it can, and it just might be your next shot!"

12. "Whatever worked today will work tomorrow."

With so many golf tips running through my head and up to four swings to choose from, it is not surprising that I occasionally try something that works. I have played great golf many times for four to six holes because of a single tweak in my game in mid-round. This happens most often on the last few holes of the day. Then, after giving my partners a parting handshake, I walk back to my car with renewed optimism, looking forward to my next round. I am anxious to see if the positive adjustment of today will carry over to tomorrow. Sadly, I have found that it won't. In my personal experience, successful tweaks are transient phenomena, similar to lunar eclipses but much less predictable. Their effects are here today and gone tomorrow. They help me catch lightning in a bottle for a few holes, but they will not work the next time I play. This truly is one of golf's mysteries. The same golfer uses the same tweak but gets the opposite result. Why? Because it's not the same day.

Now that I have exposed my inner golfing thoughts, I hope you can appreciate why I find this game so darned difficult, why I tend to play golf so badly, why I never seem to improve, and why I just might be a golf instructor's mission impossible. But I also hope you can sense how much I love the game and how hard it is to face the prospect of leaving it behind. My love of golf is the very reason I have resorted to one year of lessons. I sincerely hope my game will improve and my marriage with golf will be salvaged. But, trust me, if it doesn't get better, I am prepared to cite irreconcilable differences and walk off the course forever.

With my first lesson just around the corner, I need to set the stage by answering the following questions:

1. What courses do I play most often?

2. Which tees do I use?
3. What scoring system and rules do I follow on each course?
4. What are my lowest, highest, and average scores on these courses?
5. What clubs do I use, and how far do I hit the ball with them?
6. What recent round has made me consider giving up the game altogether?
7. How much must I improve to consider this journey a success?

The answers will be given in the next three chapters.

Chapter 4: Good Courses for Bad Golf

Four years ago, my friend Jeff complained that our busy schedules were keeping us from playing golf with each other. He and I decided our priorities needed to be adjusted, and we came up with a plan of action. We started the FedUp Cup, named after the professional FedEx Cup, for friends who were fed up with not playing golf together. Starting in the spring, we met every other Friday afternoon for a round of golf. We recorded our scores from week to week and ended the year with a FedUp Cup tournament in September. True to form, I have finished last in the FedUp standings every season of its existence.

Twin Lakes Golf Course in Arab, Alabama was our FedUp venue the first two years. When it ran into financial trouble and closed, we moved to Chesley Oaks Golf Course in nearby Fairview. The following is an overview of that course, along with the rules we established for our FedUp rounds. I will also provide my scoring history at this course while playing by these rules.

COURSE: Chesley Oaks in Fairview, Alabama
TEES PLAYED: Blue -- 6152 yards
COURSE RATING/SLOPE: 68.3/106
RULES: (1) The ball may be moved one club length
but cannot be moved closer to the hole
or into a different area (such as from
rough to fairway or fringe to green).
(2) Putts less than one foot are gimmies.

(3) Double bogey is the highest possible
score on each hole.
MY AVERAGE FED-UP SCORE: 87
MY LOWEST FED-UP SCORE: 83
MY HIGHEST FED-UP SCORE: 96

****

For the past six years, Cherokee Ridge, a golfing community twenty miles south of Huntsville, has been my place of residence and my home course. It opened in the early 1990s and quickly gained a reputation as one of the best private courses in Alabama. The Nike Tour (today's Web.com Tour) held one of its tournaments here for several years, a testimony to its championship quality. I have played many rounds of golf on this picturesque layout. Most of these have been on weekdays, playing alone or with my wife riding along (reference my two holes-in-one). Sometimes I use a cart, but just as often I push or carry my clubs.

In contrast to the generous FedUp Cup rules, I am a stickler at Cherokee Ridge when computing my score, so strict on myself it would make a USGA official proud. This, along with several course features not encountered at Chesley Oaks (sand traps, tight fairways, and out-of-bounds galore), has led to a significantly higher scoring average here. These are the details of this course and my personal history:

COURSE: Cherokee Ridge in Union Grove, Alabama
TEES PLAYED: Blue -- 6395 yards
COURSE RATING/SLOPE: 70.6/129

RULES: USGA (play it as it lies, no maximum score,
        putt everything out, etc.)
MY AVERAGE SCORE: 96
MY LOWEST SCORE: 87
MY HIGHEST SCORE: 112

****

The information above should give you an indication of what has become the golfing status quo for me. It will also serve as a baseline with which to compare my performance over the next twelve months. In addition to strokes per round, it may also be beneficial to look at my distance now versus later. My yardage with each club (when I use Swings 1-3) is given below. Anyone who knows anything about golf will instantly realize how short I am with each club in my bag. Hopefully, these yardages will rise as my scoring average falls. Until then, this is the sad tale of the tape:

driver: 205 yards
3-wood: 190 yards
5-wood: 175 yards
7-wood or 3-iron: 160 yards
9-wood or 4-iron: 150 yards
11-wood or 5-iron: 140 yards
6-iron: 130 yards
7-iron: 120 yards
8-iron: 110 yards
9-iron: 100 yards
pitching wedge: 90 yards
sand wedge: still in the trap
putter: usually, but not always, closer to the hole
ball retriever: 20 feet (with extensions)

****

Do you remember the Frosted Flakes commercial a few years back? It showed an adult sitting in a darkened room, reluctantly baring his soul. In obvious shame and in almost a whisper, he confessed, "I eat Frosted Flakes."

In the first chapters of this book, I have likewise unlocked my darkest secrets, publicly admitting, "I am a bad golfer." I have even gone a step further by giving you the shameful details of my game. Having done so, it's time for me to seek help, to undergo rehabilitation. I am now acknowledging myself as the charter member of Bad Golfers Anonymous. Like the recovering alcoholic who must avoid alcohol, the only recourse for me is to abstain from bad golf. In short, I must improve or quit. The upcoming twelve months of lessons will be my therapy sessions. Jonathan, my golfing instructor, will be my therapist. How I respond to his leadership will determine which fork (*golf* or *no golf*) I will take in the path ahead.

Before my rehab starts, there is one more question I need to answer, a question you probably have already asked at some time during my confessional. Why, after forty-plus years of bad golf, have I now come to this decision point? Why not just continue to play bad golf twenty more years and then retire? What has driven me, after a lifetime of horrible swings, to cry like Poe's raven, "Nevermore!"? What was the tipping point, the moment of clarity that finally led me to seek help? I will answer this in the next chapter.

Chapter 5: The Massacre at Shoal Creek

Someone told me a long time ago that the majority of golfers in America could not break 100 even if given several chances. I believe this is true. I have often played behind golfers who couldn't shoot in the 90s on a putt-putt course. In their defense, many of these men and women play about once a year, the golfing version of a parishioner who goes to church only on Easter Sunday. Regardless, I have prided myself that I am not in their company, that somehow I am able to maneuver my ball over eighteen holes in less than a hundred strokes. This sense of superiority over the worst of the worst has kept me playing golf and enjoying it for forty years, in spite of my own deficiencies

Comparing my game with the less fortunate, therefore, has helped me continue to play bad golf without getting too frustrated. I realize that this is somewhat akin to a 300-pound guy continuing to eat merrily because he sees a 600-pounder, but it has worked for me. I have often joked that golf is a relative game because everyone has a relative worse than him. There is some truth to this statement. I always knew I played bad golf, but I also took comfort in the fact that I was better than my dad or my brother.

Another thing that has kept me from getting too depressed about my game has been my busy schedule. I have spent my whole adult life with the fullest of plates. Every week someone would say to me, "I don't know how you do all you do!" I loved golf enough to carve out time for it, but it was never consistent. I would go three weeks without playing and then would play three times in one week. During a worse-than-average round, my playing partners would try to make me feel better by saying, "You just need to play more." I believed them. For this reason, I wasn't too hard on myself. Eventually, I predicted, I will be able to play every week and will improve. Until then, I would have to end each round the same way Walter Cronkite ended his newscasts: "That's the way it is."

This all changed in May of this year. For the first time since high school, I cut back my work schedule, freeing up time for other things. It thus became possible for me to play golf weekly, to take the game more seriously. Little did I know this would start me down a road that could lead to a golfing dead end.

As I began to expect more of myself on the golf course, my entire outlook changed from a happy-go-lucky acceptance to a do-this-or-die obsession. I made it my mission, a compulsory goal, to become a better golfer. As I set out to do this, however, I made a series of missteps that led me straight to frustration and despair. The mistakes I made (and you should avoid) are as follows:

1. I made the mistake of believing I would play better if I played more.

I should have known better from life experience. As a pastor's son and a music minister, I have heard a boatload of preachers, some good and some bad. The bad ones, I am convinced, could preach every day of the week and not improve. Given the chance to conduct a preaching marathon, they would still be able to put me to sleep quicker than my anesthesiologist. With preaching, I already knew that practice did not make perfect. Somehow I believed it would be different with golf.

2. I made the mistake of becoming my own golf instructor.

Again, I should have known better. We doctors have been warned many times not to treat ourselves. We have heard since medical school that a doctor who treats himself has a fool as his physician. With golf, I thought it would be different, so I hired myself as my golf teacher. The result: I got what I paid for and played the part of the fool.

3. I made the mistake of caring about my golf ranking within my group.

Until recently, it didn't bother me too much that I was dead last in my foursome. I figured someone had to be last, and it might as well be me. I was like a Chicago Cubs fan; it was more about the experience than about winning or losing. Taking golf seriously transformed me from Cub fan to Charlie Brown, moaning and groaning with every loss. The only difference was that the ball being teed up was round instead of oblong. With greater expectations came greater pressure to perform and greater angst when I failed. It was a sure-fire recipe for disillusionment.

4. I made the mistake of worrying about my golf ranking within my family.

The very month I started obsessing over my game, my brother firmly established himself as a better golfer. For many years I was Scott's superior on the course, but

41

he had improved and had become my equal in the last two decades. In May of this year, my commitment to improve fresh on my mind, he and I traveled to Franklin, Kentucky, the hometown of professional golfer Kenny Perry, to play the course Perry has built there. We detoured to pick up our father, just shy of his eighty-eighth birthday, so he could ride along with us.

Now Dad happens to be a *huge* Kenny Perry fan, largely because he too grew up in Kentucky and because he has developed a friendly relationship with Kenny's father. Despite being two years my father's senior, the elder Perry still helps supervise the course. A veteran of World War II, he now surveys wars of a different sort, riding from green to green each day to watch foursomes play. Ever the encourager, Mr. Perry always toots the horn of his golf cart whenever someone records a birdie. On this particular day he watched us play two holes, conversing with my father briefly each time. It almost goes without saying that he did not give me a congratulatory honk on either hole.

Our time together at Perry's golf course started well even before we got to the first tee. I let Scott and Dad off at the clubhouse and went to park my car. When I entered to join them, Dad was sitting at a small table. Directly across from him was none other than Kenny Perry himself. The two were engaged in a private conversation. I could tell by the look on Dad's face that he was in golfing heaven.

Dad seemed very comfortable conversing with his golf hero. This did not surprise me in the least, considering my father's personality. He is an extrovert who has never in his life met a stranger. No matter your status, pauper or prince, he never hesitates to go out of his way to greet you as if you are a member of his family. During my childhood and adolescence, he repeatedly introduced me to famous people we happened to encounter and did so as if *they* were the lucky ones. Because of my father's assertiveness, I have clasped the hand and stared into the eyes of a popular country comedian, Jerry Clowers; two legendary Kentucky basketball coaches, Adolph Rupp and Joe B. Hall; a hall-of-fame Wildcat basketball play-by-play announcer, Cawood Ledford; and the governors of the states of Kentucky and Tennessee. No extrovert myself, I was never enthused like Dad but openly reserved, certain that our interruption was an unwelcome intrusion into their lives.

Seeing my dad sitting down and having small talk with Kenny Perry was completely in line with his past behavior. It was sheer luck that Perry was taking a week off from his tournament schedule on the Champion's Tour and that he was in the clubhouse at that moment. What made this encounter extra special was my father's twenty-year infatuation with the man sitting across from him. Week after week, Dad had celebrated Perry's triumphs and agonized over his defeats. To meet him in person was a victory in itself.

"Kenny Perry, this is my doctor son, Randy," Dad said, as I entered the clubhouse. His voice was upbeat, his countenance uplifted.

Perry, his unshaven face testifying to a much needed day off, smiled and said hello.

43

"Kenny," I replied, "I feel like I am meeting the third son my father never had. He is perhaps your greatest fan."

What followed was a ten-minute conversation about a variety of topics. If Perry felt put out, he never showed it. He was the ultimate gentleman, a tribute to his upbringing and his country roots. I'm sure it helped that our dads were peers in age and friendly acquaintances.

As our tee time approached, Dad was still sitting there engrossed in conversation, time standing still "Dad," I interrupted, "do you think I can pull you away from Kenny long enough to watch your sons play?"

He obliged, but not before looking straight at Perry to tell him, "You are one of my heroes!"

For Dad, the remainder of the day was icing on the cake. For me, it was a desert instead of a dessert. I promptly shot 101 and watched my brother play one of the best rounds of his life, shooting 85. It was obvious that the torch of "best golfer in the family" had been passed to Scott. Since Dad had retired from golf, I became the family's "worst golfer" that day. It was a humiliating way to start my quest for improvement, an initial salvo that sent my confidence reeling.

5. I made the mistake of comparing my present game with my past.

Besides being the worst golfer in my group and family, it became obvious in June of this year that I was also the worst golfer in my own life. Compared with my former years, I was inferior. In a foursome consisting of

Randy Stewart during each of my four decades of golf, the 2014 version would be at the bottom of the leaderboard. I would not make the cut today.

I am about to share the unpleasant details of my fall from grace in June, during which I played more rounds of golf than ever before. Before I do, allow me to give you some friendly advice. Please take some ibuprofen and a find a comfortable seat. This could be long and painful.

During the first week of June, my wife and I traveled to Georgia for an expenses-paid getaway, a parting gift from our church after I resigned as music minister. The two-night, three-day romantic package to Chateau Élan Winery and Resort seemed odd for a couple of reasons. For one thing, the gift was from a Southern Baptist church that has a long anti-alcohol position. In fact, our church had twice led the fight against legalizing alcohol sales in the city. When I received the gift certificate to the winery—in front of the entire congregation—I kept the details confidential and laughed inside. I knew that someone had purchased this without approval from the church leadership. That my wife and I are teetotalers made the gift seem all the more out of place. Although we do not consider social drinking an absolute no-no, we do not consume alcohol in any form and have no desire to change. When we made our reservation and were told that a bottle of champagne would await us in our room upon arrival, we requested and were granted another treat. Upon entering the suite, we located our celebratory beverage smugly chilling in the small refrigerator. We then toasted the beginning of our time of romance by downing two cans of Diet Coke.

45

The real reason the church sent us there was the golf, not the wine. The resort boasted three beautiful courses, two of these open to the public. I played a round on both. The first eighteen holes were bad; the second were horrible. I had decided that in order to improve I had to become a longer striker of the ball. I therefore spent those thirty-six holes trying every conceivable way to hit my ball farther. I succeeded: it went farther right then farther left, farther into the lake and farther into the woods. I left Chateau Élan more infatuated with my wife but more infuriated with my game.

During the middle of June we traveled to Orange Beach, Alabama, again for three days. I played two more rounds there, the first on an Arnold Palmer design in Foley called Cotton Creek. I was paired with a husband and wife from Houston, Texas who were in their early seventies. True to form, his game in my presence ascended to new heights. After birdies on two of the first five holes, I overheard him say to his wife, "I don't know what golfer has taken over my body!" I shook my head, walked to my cart, recorded double bogey on my scorecard, and cursed the gods of golf. Although the gentleman started having swing problems on the back nine, he never descended to the depths of golfing torment that I endured. I can't recall my score that day, but I know it was a triple-digit number.

The next day I took on the challenge of Lost Key Golf Course in Pensacola, Florida. It is touted as one of the most difficult in the area, with a course rating just over 74. I found it tight and loaded with hazards, just as advertised. Even though I played a little better ("not as bad" would be a more accurate description), the unique perils of Lost Key made the day just as frustrating. Want to know how bad it got? Despite playing alone, a trailing twosome accused me of slow play. I am ashamed to confess that I lost more than several golf balls that day. I lost my cool as well. The only consolation was a score of 97, not too bad under the circumstances.

After the four rounds above, it was becoming more and more obvious to me that my golf game was not improving. In fact, it was slipping in the opposite direction. Determined not to fail, I returned home to Union Grove and played three more rounds at Cherokee Ridge. I decided not to keep score, instead focusing on making changes to my swing that would improve both distance and direction. I felt some added pressure during these days as I tweaked my game, for I knew that another golfing trip awaited me, this time to the most prestigious course in the state. I looked forward to it as an opportunity to continue my pursuit of excellence. As it turned out, this would be the round that would compel me to seek a new instructor. I would fire myself that day, with good reason.

6. I made the mistake of playing Shoal Creek near Birmingham with my game already teetering on the brink of collapse.

It did collapse that day, and with it any golfing self-esteem remaining in my body. It seemed as if every recurring theme of my golfing career reared its ugly head, that the ghosts of rounds past decided to hold a convention on the most hallowed golfing ground in Alabama and chose me as the topic of the day. When I left the course, I was a defeated and embarrassed man. Golf was no longer enjoyable, and I did not want to play anymore. If this was to be my future, golfing would be my past.

Shoal Creek is a Jack Nicklaus design nestled in Hoover, on the outskirts of Birmingham's metropolitan area. It has twice been the site of the year's fourth major (the PGA Championship), is presently the home of The Tradition (one of the majors on the Champion's Tour), and is scheduled to host the U.S. Women's Open in 2018. This is all you need to know to understand that it is a cut above the rest. Its reputation among professional golfers is outstanding. I have heard from a reliable source that Tom Watson agreed to play in The Tradition a few years ago only if Shoal Creek was the venue.

With rich history, superb reputation, and private membership, Shoal Creek is not easily accessible. Tee times must be scheduled by a member, who is also required to be one of the foursome. Carts are forbidden and caddies are mandatory, driving the cost of a round of golf over the two hundred dollar mark. My connection to play here is my son-in-law Alan, whose parents are members. Prior to last month, I had played Shoal Creek twice. Both were related to Alan and Allison's wedding. It was on the eighteenth tee, in fact, that Alan asked me if he could marry her. A few weeks later, I was there again as part of his "final bachelor weekend" festivities.

I had promised one of my physician friends that I would arrange a round of golf at Shoal Creek. One call to Larry, Alan's dad, and the date was set. The morning of June 26, Larry and I met my friend Craig at the practice range. With Craig was Keith, one of his Guntersville golfing buddies. The four of us were assigned two caddies. One, a thin African-American with more than

48

three decades of caddying experience, toted the bags of Craig and Keith. The other, a stout young man from Wisconsin, was Larry's caddy and mine. Bags in tow, they led the four of us to the first tee.

Larry and I elected to play from the tees closest to 6000 yards. Craig and Keith, longer and straighter, moved back one set. On hole #1, a par four, I promptly recorded a seven, primarily the result of two failed attempts to get out of a greenside bunker. Somehow I recovered on the par-four second hole with a par. Other than a near-birdie on the par-three sixth, the rest of the day was catastrophic. All of hell's fury was unleashed on me as a host of golfing demons tormented my mind, body, and spirit. The individual holes are now a blur, but several general themes of the round remain painfully clear. As I noted above, they are representative of every unpleasant golfing experience in my lifetime.

A magnet for advice. It didn't take long for my caddy to recognize my deficiencies. By the third hole he was offering advice, once even taking the club out of my hand to show me how to swing. He continued in instruction mode the majority of the round. Only on the eighteenth hole, when he realized that I was beyond help, did he revert only to caddying.

A lack of distance. My poor caddy could not believe the yardages I hit my clubs. In fact, he would have none of it. I would tell him I wanted a 6-iron; he would hand me an eight. When I preferred a 7-wood, he suggested a 5-iron. Trying not to be more troublesome than I already was, I complied with his advice. You can imagine the results. My ball flight began to be as random as a bottle rocket, sometimes left and sometimes right, sometimes high and sometimes low, sometimes short and sometimes long. Eventually I told the caddy not to second-guess my club selection, but by then I was a basket case. Every club in my bag was a dud.

A variety of swings. During that day, I ran the gamut of the swings at my disposal. By the back nine, I had canned Swings 1-3 and had resorted to the foreshortened Swing #4. If my caddy had trouble with my distances before, imagine his reaction then. It seems to me that I might have invented a couple of new swings during the round. I can't be sure, since individual swings are now a blur.

A witness to greatness. None of us played to his potential that day, but this didn't stop my partners from performing golfing feats bordering on the incredible. On one par five, Keith holed out from sixty yards away. On another hole, after he hit a low liner into a water hazard, I watched in awe as the ball skipped five times on the water's surface and landed on the opposite bank on dry land. After an up-and-down, he recorded his score: a par. Craig also had a skip-over-the-water-onto-dry-land shot, although not as amazing as Keith's. Larry holed the day's longest putt, a winding double-breaker that he would normally sink once in fifty tries. As for me, I was relegated to being a spectator of the miraculous. The law of averages apparently cannot afford a round at Shoal Creek.

A bogey putter *par excellence*. Par putts were rare that day, but as usual I missed every one of them greater than a tap-in. Bogey putts were plentiful, putts for double bogey even more so. These were struck with the calmness and precision of a neurosurgeon. I am now convinced my putter is possessed with par-putt-itis, a rare and incurable disease linked somehow to a golfer's brain and hands, leading to uncontrollable tremors on short putts for par. If this condition doesn't improve, it might be time to put my putter in a nursing home.

A habitual cellar dweller. Once again, I finished last. Larry tried his best to play worse than me, but in the end he could not hit enough bad shots to earn last place. The fact that he was approaching his seventieth birthday and was playing with a bad back did not help my feelings. His bad back was no match for my bad game.

A triple-digit mathematician. I'm not quite sure what I shot that day. We played as teams, Larry and I against Craig and Keith, so we didn't focus on individual scoring. It was good that we didn't. If I had to venture a guess, I shot somewhere in the mid-120s, thanks to a rare good day at the beach. (I got out of seven of eight bunkers in one shot). If not for this, my score would have exceeded 130. That's worse than triple-bogey golf, and that, my friends, is very, very bad.

An honest accountant. If you add green fees, caddy fees and tips, lunch at the clubhouse, and gasoline to and fro, I spent a grand total of $250 that day to play at Shoal Creek. That's two dollars per stroke and fourteen dollars per hole, inflated statistics that would make even Donald Trump give pause. If I had never previously played the course, it might have been worth it. Since I had, it was nothing less than masochistic extravagance, similar to paying top dollar for your own execution.

****

That afternoon, as I exited the gates of Shoal Creek, the security officer guarding the torture chamber gave me a friendly parting wave. As far as I was concerned, he might as well have been telling my golf game goodbye. At that moment I hated golf, everything about it. I hated my clubs, especially my short irons. I hated my swing(s). I was not too fond of my caddy, to whom I had just handed an extra $25 (a 33% tip). I hated Shoal Creek and all golf courses, manicured minefields inflicting more agony than the devil and Obamacare combined. Most of all, I hated my instructor and his pupil. In other words, I hated my golfing self.

It was at that very moment, less than a mile removed from the entrance to Shoal Creek, that the light came on.

An inner voice, almost audible, cut through the hate-filled fog: "Get better or quit!"

No longer able to exert my own will, I nodded and spoke aloud. "I agree."

The inner voice continued. "You can't do it by yourself."

"I know," I replied, "but I'm not so sure I can do it even with someone's help."

"Might as well try," the voice within advised. "What have you got to lose?"

Without thinking, I answered: "Just my future as a golfer."

Then I began to think about it. A cold chill ran down my spine as I considered the possibility of giving up golf forever. It had not happened yet, but I already found myself mourning the game I had played so poorly yet loved so deeply.

The choice before me was as clear as day. The dreadful events at Shoal Creek were too fresh and raw to consider the possibility of playing my game where it laid. Maintaining the status quo, therefore, was too painful an option. But so was quitting. There was only one possible path to contentment.

"I have to become a better golfer," I said, for once really meaning it.

The next thing I did was grab my phone to email someone who could help.

Chapter 6: The Week Before

On June 26, 2014 at 2:53 pm, the Shoal Creek Massacre just one hour in my rearview mirror, I typed and sent the following email:

Jonathan,

For the first time in my life I have enough free time to take some golf lessons and do the necessary "homework" on the range. I'm looking for someone to teach me an hour each week for one year. I want to start from the beginning and learn how to do things correctly instead of trying to tweak a bad golf swing. Would you be interested and have the time? If not, whom would you recommend? I'm ready to start next week. Goodbye, shanks!

Randy

I have known Jonathan since he was a young boy. His father, Ron, and I served at the same church in the early 1990s as ministers of education and music, respectively, and have continued to keep in touch, mostly through golf. (He has been one of our FedUp Cup participants every year.) He is one of the most likable, humble, and dedicated Christians I know, and I'm not saying this just because my golf teacher is his son.

Jonathan is the eldest of Ron's three boys. If my recollection is correct, he played on our high school golf team. He also experimented with tennis, occasionally challenging my daughters to a friendly grudge match. When he moved away to attend college and start a career, I lost touch with him.

One day, while playing golf together, I asked Ron what Jonathan was up to. I learned that he was married, was living in Georgia, and was the head golf professional at a country club. That last piece of information was a bit surprising to me. I remembered Jonathan being an above-average high school golfer but nowhere near a certified professional. I didn't think he was that good.

I soon found out how wrong I was. On one of Jonathan's visits home to Alabama, I played in a foursome that included him. To say the least, I was impressed. Other than two PGA Championship rounds at Shoal Creek, his golf that day was the finest I had ever witnessed. That little sucker, no more than five feet and six inches tall in brand new spikes, had more distance than a truck driver, a better short game than a turtle, a hotter flat blade than the cook at Waffle House, more successful up-and-downs than an Olympic gymnast, and as many birdies as a badminton tournament. He shot less than 70 that afternoon, and it seemed as effortless as a hang glider in flight. Even though I wasn't privy to all that had happened to him during his time away, I knew that somewhere on a golf course he had made the trans-formation from Clark Kent to Superman.

Like all good golfers, Jonathan was quick to offer help when he saw the pitiful state of my game. He noticed how I sliced everything except my putts, and he promised that he could help me overcome this. He was right. In just one short lesson, he had me hitting the ball straight, sometimes even right to left. Unlike so many changes to my game, this cure was permanent. Habitual slicing never again was a problem for me. Unfortunately, we did not have time for lesson two. Faster than a speeding bullet, Jonathan was off to Georgia again.

I learned two important things about Jonathan that weekend: he was an excellent golfer and an excellent golf teacher. Trust me, it's not always so. There are many great golfers out there who would have a hard time teaching Iron Byron how to swing, much less a golfer as flawed as yours truly.

I learned this the hard way about five years ago when my daughters gave me twelve golf lessons with a well-known company. I am confident that my instructor could strike the ball as well as Jonathan, but his teaching skills were those of a hacker. Every lesson he would attach wires to my body to measure my rotation and clubhead speed and would point video cameras at me to compare my swing with other golfers. Which golfers? I'm glad you asked. On a split screen, my swing was measured against that of Tiger Woods, Stuart Appleby, Ernie Els, and Davis Love III. I was told to copy their address, takeaway, backswing, downswing, impact, and follow-through. You might as well have told me to join a Cirque du Soleil. Their spines torqued, their muscles flexed, and their bodies contorted in ways impossible for me to imitate. After nine sessions with this teacher and his method, my game did not improve one stroke, and I ached from head to toe. Foregoing the final three lessons, I bid Tiger and his pals farewell.

With Jonathan, it was different. We had only one session together, but in this brief experience he proved his talent as a golfing mentor. Like a kindergarten teacher with the ABCs, he started with me at the basics and then built upon them. By the end of those two hours of instruction, I was much farther along (and less sore) than after nine weeks with that other guy. Given more time, I was certain Jonathan could lead me to the bliss of golfing respectability. Unfortunately, he lived in Georgia, so the chance of it happening was slim.

This all changed, however, when he moved back to Alabama. The long hours as a club professional had begun to take their toll, conflicting with his commitment to family and church. Consequently, he decided to retire from golf administration, returning with his wife and two daughters to his hometown. He petitioned the USGA to have his status as a golf professional repealed and received written confirmation when this was granted. He now describes himself as a certified, card-carrying amateur.

You can understand now why Jonathan was the person I turned to when I gave myself that golfing ultimatum. I knew firsthand how gifted an instructor he was, how in a short time he had miraculously cured my slice. I also remembered his offer to give me additional lessons when the timing was right. That's why I emailed him and no one else. I needed a golfing Moses to lead me out of bondage, and he fit the description perfectly.

After a few minutes of anxious waiting, I received his reply:

> You bet! It would be my honor. Just let me know what day you would like to begin this week and what time you have in mind. We can start with, "This is a golf club..." if you like.

Hope swelled within me as I read his response. After many rocky years together, my clubs and I need a fresh start, perhaps even some arbitration. Jonathan seems the perfect person to mediate our differences. Our first lesson together is set for tomorrow at Cherokee Ridge. It is difficult for me to describe how much I am looking forward to it. Imagine a trapped coal miner as he hears the sounds of his approaching rescuer, and you will get some idea.

Chapter 7: Home Off the Range (Lesson 1)

I failed to mention in the last chapter that I bought a couple of golf instructional books on the way home from Shoal Creek. I was afraid my game would be so foreign to Jonathan that he would have trouble communicating with me. To help move things along, I needed some rudimentary knowledge of proper golfing technique and psychology.

With this in mind, I headed to the sports section at Books-a-Million and purchased two golf references. One was *Golf My Way*, a best-selling analysis of the golf swing by Jack Nicklaus. I figured if anyone would know proper form, the greatest golfer of all time would be the man. The other book, *The Inner Game of Golf*, was written by a tennis player who was able to break 80 merely by tuning his mental game. I chose this because his quest for improvement seemed similar to mine.

Later that day, as I began reading the two books, I discovered an odd coincidence: both were written in 1974, the same year I graduated from high school. Believe it or not, this made me feel better going into my first lesson. I considered it a sign from heaven that I was pursuing the right path and that the golfing planets were aligning just for me. In retrospect, however, I was being a tad bit superstitious. Only desperate people see such things as signs. The sick, dehydrated, thirsty traveler is the one who sees the mirage in the desert. The healthy person does not.

Desperate or not, I arrived at Cherokee Ridge Golf Course thirty minutes early for my first lesson. While I waited for Jonathan, I decided to go to the driving range to hit a few balls. This was bizarre behavior, if you think about it. Why would someone practice his swing a half hour before beginning a swing overhaul? It's about as irrational as a woman cleaning her dilapidated house just before the city demolishes it. But there I was, alone on the range, flailing away with a 7-iron.

After about ten minutes, I was joined on the practice facility by Adam, one of the best golfers at our course. He found a place a few slots down from me and started hitting balls, too. We didn't have much to say to each other, at least initially. Even though I knew who he was, we had never previously had a one-minute conversation.

If you remember how I tend to attract golfing advice, you will not be surprised that Adam and I soon established a mentor-pupil relationship. By the time Jonathan arrived, this tall, lanky scratch golfer was serving as the warm-up act, giving me a few helpful hints. If I wasn't convinced yet that my swing was atrocious, his spontaneous, unsolicited instruction left no doubt that I was the golfing equivalent of a monotone. At that moment, there was not one thing about my game that I wanted to keep as a souvenir. When Jonathan stepped to the range and offered me his hand, I threw my 7-iron at his feet and begged for mercy and deliverance.

After a few pleasantries, we began lesson one. The location Jonathan chose was not what I expected. I had waited for him on the driving range because I assumed this is where we would start. What better place could there be to diagnose and treat my golfing ailments? My new teacher had other plans.

"Let's start down there," he said, pointing to the practice putting green a few yards away.

I followed him and watched as he dumped about twenty balls into the light rough about five yards from the putting surface. He then handed my pitching wedge to me and explained my first assignment.

"Chip these balls to that hole, the one closest to us."

I felt a little nervous as I began to chip balls toward the short flag just twelve yards away. Jonathan watched, not saying a word, which made me even more nervous. After a couple of minutes, he told me to stop and then walked onto the putting service to do some quick math.

"You've just hit ten chips from less than fifteen yards, and seven are on the green. That means that thirty percent of your short-range chips don't even reach the putting surface."

His tone was not in any way condescending or demeaning. He was sympathetic but also matter-of-fact, leaving no doubt that a seventy-percent success rate from this distance was not satisfactory. Even though I didn't voice it, I considered this first exercise somewhat a waste of time. If Jonathan wanted to convince me that I was horrible around the green, he was about six weeks late.

Apparently having proved his point, Jonathan next reached for an encyclopedia-sized book and got right to the theme of lesson one.

"I know that you see great golfers on TV, and it looks like their swings are different. In some ways they are, but they are also alike in other respects. The choppy swings of Lee Trevino and Arnold Palmer may seem opposite of the fluid swings of Ernie Els and Adam Scott, but if you look at certain stages of their swings, they do things the same. The sooner you realize this and copy those similarities, the sooner you will become a better golfer."

I was not sure I believed what he said. It seemed to me that Trevino and Els were not very similar during any part of their swings. As if sensing my doubt, Jonathan opened the book and stepped toward me to prove his point.

"Look at these golfers from the early 1900s through today. Every one of these pictures is taken at the point of impact with the ball. Do they look the same or different?"

"They look the same," I replied. Indeed, the photos proved that the impact positions of these famous male and female golfers were virtually identical.

Jonathan continued: "Great golfers may do some things differently before impact, but by the time the club hits the ball they all are singing the same song. So your question today is this: what do these great golfers have in common at address and how do I join them?"

He turned the book toward me even more. It was obvious that he was about to make an important teaching point.

"Look at their hands in relation to the clubhead. Every great golfer, now and one hundred years ago, has his or her hands in front of the ball at impact. Put another way, the clubface is behind the hands when it comes in contact with the ball. This is core knowledge point #1: your hands should be in front of the ball at impact on all golf shots, from the driver to the putter."

"And mine aren't?" I asked, almost rhetorically.

"Not even close," he replied. "Let's see if we can change that."

I spent the remainder of the lesson chipping from that same spot near the practice green, my only goal being to get my hands in front of the ball at impact. It is hard for me to exaggerate how foreign this was. Apparently, I had always been a "flipper" (Jonathan's term), someone who flips both wrists prior to impact and thus moves the clubface ahead of the hands. Trying to change this four-decade habit in thirty minutes was extremely difficult. It was like handing chopsticks to a man who had eaten with a fork for forty years and saying, "Let me watch you eat those peas." Messy is one word that comes close to describing my first attempts. But, to my surprise, by the end of the session I was beginning to get my hands in front of the clubhead at impact and —better yet, according to Jonathan—was beginning to feel when I failed to do so.

"You don't learn to play," he said. "You play to learn, just like you're doing here today. You are practicing your chips with a goal in mind: hands in front of the clubface at impact. That is your assignment this week. Avoid the driving range. Chip to these five holes on the practice green with that goal in mind."

In addition to core knowledge point #1, I also learned four sub-points today. The first is to keep my wrists from breaking down (i.e. bending) after impact. The second is to keep my lower body and head relatively still. The third is to let my upper arms and shoulders be the primary muscle-movers. The fourth is to contact the ball with a downward blow rather than a level or upward blow. In Jonathan's terminology, I am to be a digger, not a sweeper.

Thankfully, I discovered today that I don't have to think about all of these sub-points at the same time. If I concentrate on the main point (my hands being ahead of the clubface at impact), the sub-points naturally fall into place. If I get my hands out in front, my wrists are less likely to bend after impact, my lower body and head are less likely to roam, my upper arms and shoulders are more prone to lead, and my impact is more likely to be a downward blow. This is not true 100% of the time, but it is consistent enough to keep me focused on the main thing: hands out in front at impact.

I'm glad that this is so. Chipping is hard enough with one thought swimming around in my head as I move the club. It would be torture if I had to think about all the sub-points, too. Consider a paratrooper in mid-air. If he worries too much about his stunts, jumpsuit, the weather, etc., he just might forget to pull the ripcord, with disastrous results. In like manner, I should not become so enamored with the sub-points of a golf swing that I neglect the main point of focus. If I do, my ball, like that parachutist, will have an unpleasant landing.

Until my next lesson, then, I will focus my attention solely on the location of my hands relative to the clubface at impact. To change such an ingrained fault will require all my concentration. For over forty years, the position of my hands and clubhead at contact has been opposite of all great golfers. This has to be one of the main reasons the words "great" and "golfer" have never appeared in the same sentence about me.

Chapter 8: The Full Swing (Lesson 2)

After my first lesson, chipping to the practice green became my lone golfing activity and getting my hands in front of the clubface at impact my only swing thought. This hands-first move was a fascinating concept to me. I thought about it a lot, maybe too much, and started seeing a similar pattern in other daily activities. When I brushed my teeth, I noticed that my hand was always in front of my toothbrush. When I swept the sidewalk, the broom seemed to work best if my hands led the bristles and I attacked the dirt with a downward stroke. At times, this obsession approached the borders of mental illness. As I walked hand-in-hand in the sunset hours with my wife, I placed my hand ahead of hers. At night, when changing TV channels, I made sure the back of my hand was closer to the screen than the remote control. When I read my Bible at bedtime, I would turn to a higher page number with my left hand and to a lower page number with my right, so that my hand would always lead the paper. I would then say my nighttime prayer with hands clasped in front of me, wrists locked, my head relatively motionless.

By my second lesson, therefore, I had pretty much mastered the hands-in-front move. It became less and less forced, more and more natural. To be honest, my chipping was not much better, but I didn't let this bother me. Better chipping was not my homework assignment; getting my hands in front of the ball at impact was. If I did my homework well, Jonathan promised, improvement would come over time. Through repetition, I would eventually learn from my successes and mistakes. But he was adamant that this would happen only if I mastered the position of my hands relative to the ball at impact.

I assumed we would continue to tweak the short chip in lesson two, but I discovered I was wrong again when I got this text message: *Meet me at Chesley Oaks. I'll be at the far end of the driving range.*

When I arrived, Jonathan was killing time by hitting a few balls. I watched as I walked toward him, wondering how a swing so smooth by a man so compact could launch a golf ball so far. By the end of our hour together, I would know some of the reasons why.

"Take your 7-iron and hit a few balls toward that red flag," Jonathan said. "As you do, I want you to focus once more on core knowledge point #1: hands in front of the ball at impact."

I noticed that the number of balls Jonathan had with him was much greater than the previous week. He must have read my mind. "By the end of this lesson, you may be a little sore."

He watched me intently as I struck about twenty balls. I tried my best to do so with my hands leading the way, but I wasn't certain I was succeeding. The feel of the full swing was different than that of the chip.

"Are my hands out in front?" I asked.

"You bet!" he replied. "I can tell you have been practicing a lot since last week."

Hearing my young mentor compliment my work ethic was encouraging and energizing. It was the first time in my life a great golfer had said anything good about my game. I realize he was merely acknowledging that I had done my homework, but the effect on me was similar to the moment my wife first told me I was handsome. I soaked it in like a sponge.

My euphoria was short-lived. Jonathan promptly followed his positive affirmation with a negative critique of my grip. It was not what he wanted, and I had to change it. As I would soon discover, it was the first of several alterations he would make today.

"Grip the club like you usually do and take your stance at address," he began. "Now rotate your left hand counter-clockwise so that you can see the knuckles of your index, middle, and ring fingers."

I did as instructed. The net effect was to have the back of my left hand directed not too high (to the sky) or too low (toward the target) but halfway between. Before this change, it was aimed almost directly at my target.

"Keep your left hand where it is and remove your right hand," he continued. "Now replace your right hand on the club so that the grip rests just below your fingers, along the palm side of your knuckles."

Again, I complied. The club no longer sat in the center of my right palm, as had been the case for forty years. It was farther down, nearer my fingers. Unlike the back of my left hand, my right palm now pretty much faced the target. As you might have guessed, this seemed a bit awkward at first. After a few swings, however, I was pleasantly surprised how natural and powerful it felt.

I read somewhere that Jesus came to afflict the comfortable and to comfort the afflicted. It was obvious that my golfing messiah was doing the same. Whenever I struggled with a swing change, he would give me reassurance. As soon as he sensed I was comfortable, he would immediately afflict me with something new.

"You seem to like the new grip," he observed. "Now let's work on your body posture."

What followed was an odd dance between Jonathan and me. I again assumed my address position, holding the club with my new grip. Taking the lead, Jonathan moved both of my upper arms inward so that they touched the sides of my chest. This felt stranger than the grip change, almost as foreign as last week when I tried to get my hands in front of the ball. The best way I can describe this arm position would be the way a penguin would have to hold a club. (I now believe penguins migrated to a land without golf courses to avoid having to swing a golf club this way. Consistent with this theory, I am coining a new golf term today. One under par is a birdie. Two under par is an eagle. A quadruple bogey is now a penguin.)

Continuing the "let's change your posture" polka, Jonathan next asked me to push my belt buckle a little farther away from the ball, which is a Christian way of saying, "Stick your butt out more!"

I now resembled a penguin with a hemorrhoid problem.

"That's so much better!" Jonathan exclaimed. It was the most excited tone of voice I had yet heard from him. "You now look like you are ready to swing a golf club. Go ahead, try it."

Despite the fact that I felt like a golfer ready to get a prostate exam, I began to hit balls with my new grip and posture. The results were, to say the least, inconsistent, although I did launch a few balls with my 7-iron farther than ever before.

Jonathan again seemed satisfied. "Two more changes today, then we are done. They both have to do with your backswing. First, try to rotate your left shoulder so that it ends up behind the ball. Second, try to keep your left arm straight throughout the backswing. Don't bend it."

I rehearsed this a few times, making sure I turned my left shoulder beyond the ball and kept my left arm straight. This required more shoulder rotation than I had ever attempted during four decades of backswings. Likewise, the unbent left elbow was something I had never considered or attempted. As I took the club back this way, I noticed a tension in my upper torso similar to a coiled spring. I also sensed some stored up power ready to be unleashed.

"Now put it all together and see what happens," Jonathan said.

Gripping the club correctly, I assumed the awkward posture, made the backswing with rotated left shoulder and unbent left elbow, and struck the ball with my hands out in front. I did so for about ten minutes, alternating between several clubs Jonathan handed me. Once again I sprayed shots all over the range, but a few times everything seemed to click. When it did, I felt a golfing sensation I had never before experienced. The ball seemed to explode off the clubface, traveling twenty yards farther than ever before and on a lower trajectory than I was accustomed to.

The first time it happened, I looked at Jonathan and said, "That was different. How did I do that?"

"You compressed the golf ball," he explained.

I had heard the term "compression" over the years but had never understood it, much less accomplished it. To my simple mind, the golf ball was as hard as a rock and could not be reshaped, no matter how tightly I squeezed it. Recently, however, I was forced to conclude that I was wrong. During lesson one, Jonathan had shown me some close-up pictures (in that encyclopedia-sized book) of a driver head contacting the ball. These pictures were proof that compression is not a myth. One side of the ball, the impact side, was caved in by the force of the clubface. This produced a trampoline effect that shot the ball off the face like a rocket.

Having experienced my first ball compression, Jonathan explained to me why it was an important milestone. "This is one of the main reasons we've made all these adjustments to your swing. Good posture at address, shoulder rotation and straight left arm during the backswing, and forward hand position at impact are all critical if you want to compress the ball. And, believe me, you really do need to compress the ball for maximum distance."

I wanted to make sure I understood. "So two golfers could hit an identical brand of golf ball with identical clubs in identical weather conditions on identical flight paths with identical clubhead speed but have different distances?"

"That would be true," Jonathan answered, "if one golfer compressed the ball and the other didn't. I want you to be the golfer who does. Don't forget how it felt today when you compressed the ball. We want this to become the rule, not the exception. Practice everything you learned the last two weeks with this goal in mind. Let's call it a day."

****

Before we proceed to lesson three, can I make a disclaimer? What I am sharing with you is a personal testimony of my own golf journey. It is in no way intended to serve as instruction to other golfers. The thought that I could help someone's game, even indirectly, is laughable. A penguin has no right to teach another winged creature how to fly.

This leads me to one final point: it's way too early to declare victory. In spite of the progress I have made in lessons one and two, I still have no idea where this will end. My shots are as erratic as ever. My short game is as lousy as a month ago. The worst parts of my game —putting, pitching, and sand shots—haven't even been discussed. Moreover, I have yet to take my new swing to the golf course and thus have no guarantee it will yield lower scores.

If it doesn't, I will not waver from my promise to walk away from the game, no matter how pretty and powerful I look at address. Unless I improve on the course by next July, I will never again grip a club or try to compress a ball. I will add *golf* to my list of four-letter words. Like that tuxedoed fowl at the frozen tundra, I will permanently retreat from the game.

Chapter 9: Putting 101 (Lesson 3)

I divided my time between the range and the practice green after my second lesson. Chipping seemed even more difficult with the new grip and posture, but I was a faithful student and did not deviate from my instructions. Hitting woods and medium-to-long irons became easier. The times I compressed the ball and sent it soaring became more frequent.

My short irons, however, remained my greatest nemesis. Even with a new grip, posture, backswing, and impact position, watching me strike a golf ball with a 9-iron was painful. With my pitching wedge, it was even worse. I am not trying to embellish when I tell you that I now regard that wedge as my bitter enemy. It is a prodigal that does not obey the laws of golf physics. Its sole reason for existing is to inflict agony and insult on poor pitiful me.

****

Jonathan and I were back at the practice green for lesson three. He first observed me hit a few chip shots and again applauded my hand position at impact. He had some comments and advice but made no major changes.

Next it was on to the putting surface.

Jonathan's first objective was to help me realize the importance of the putt. "If you shoot 100," he asserted, "I bet you average over forty putts a round."

The number seemed a little high, so I asked him to clarify. "Are you counting a putt only when the ball is on the putting surface, like the pros do, or do you also count when the putter is used from the fringe or just off the green?"

"Any time you use a putter, it's a putt," he replied. "And I am guessing you do that forty times a round."

Some quick math confirmed his suspicion. Two-putting every green would be thirty-six putts, but I rarely accomplish this. Even if I throw in a couple of one-putts, I probably do reach for the flat blade forty times in eighteen holes.

"What is your own personal goal, Jonathan?" I asked.

"Less than thirty putts a round," he said, "and I am successful more often than not. If one of your dreams is to break 90 consistently, become a good putter. Putting less than thirty times would cut more than ten strokes off your score and put you in the high 80s. And that's true if you didn't change one thing about the rest of your game."

Jonathan's pre-putt speech was reminiscent of Knute Rockne and Bear Bryant. I salivated as I listened, visualizing my scorecard with an 88 or lower every time I played. By the time he finished, I was ready to charge the practice green and attack every cup, no matter the cost. I wanted to impress my coach, to lay it all on the line for him. I knew that a three-putt would put a frown on his face the same way a fumble once did to Vince Lombardi.

Coach Jonathan, not quite ready to unleash the beast, continued his pep talk. "Before I let you start, I need to emphasize that we will concentrate today almost entirely on putts of six feet or less. These are the putts that will make or break you. If you master your putting stroke within this range, your score will plummet. Think about it a second. The shorter the putt, the greater chance you have of sinking it. So why waste your time on a twenty-foot putt? PGA professionals sink less than 20% from this distance. Common sense says that you should concentrate on perfecting your putting game from six feet in. This will pay huge dividends on the golf course."

Jonathan was true to his word. For the next twenty minutes he watched me try to make putts of six feet or less. Along the way, he made some suggestions:

1. "Grip the putter so that your thumbs run straight down the shaft. This squares up your palms to the putting line. Have you noticed the top side of your putting grip? It is flat. A lot of companies make putters this way so your thumbs have a comfortable and correct place to rest."

2. "Some golf professionals advocate taking the putterhead straight back and through on the target line. Others favor a takeaway and follow-through on an arc with the head square only at address and impact. I am a big fan of moving the putter blade along an arc. It's a natural move that mimics what happens in the full swing. Straight back and straight through is not natural. In fact, studies have shown that it is impossible for the majority of golfers, even professionals, to perfect this."

3. "Elbows out is a horrible way to putt. To avoid this, keep your upper arms, especially your left

79

arm, near the sides of your chest, just like you now do when you address the ball on the full swing." (My immediate thought: "Coming to a putting green near you: *Return of the Penguin*.")

4. "Your arms move; your body doesn't. I want you to focus on the second highest button on your shirt. It should not move at all during the entire putting stroke."

5. "Concentrate on your distance on these short putts. Imagine a penny at the back of the cup. Try to roll the ball on the line you've chosen so that it would stop just past that penny. If you do this, you'll be surprised how many times the hole will get in the way."

6. "Hit the putt first; look at the ball later. If you lift or turn your head too soon, both direction and distance on your putts will be inconsistent."

I tried to concentrate on all these points as I putted, but I discovered it was almost impossible to do so. If I focused on my upper arms, my shirt button would move. If I made sure my head did not lift too soon, my elbows would often drift from my chest. Mastering the art of putting was not going to be a quick fix.

During the last part of the lesson, Jonathan had me try a combined chipping and putting drill. He placed six golf balls in a circle, each of them three feet away from the hole. My mission was to chip balls inside this circle. If I did, it was considered a par. If I didn't, I had to putt that ball out. His goal was to emphasize how my score could drop the fastest.

"If you can chip a ball inside this six-foot diameter, three feet on each side of the cup, and if you become automatic from three feet in, I guarantee you will break 90. Let's pretend these next eighteen chips and putts are eighteen holes of golf. Try to get inside that three-foot range."

Knowing that we were keeping score meant there was added pressure on me. This added pressure, as usual, yielded inconsistent results. I don't recall my score, but I do know that I did not chip or putt as well in this exercise as I did during previous sessions with Jonathan or when I practiced alone. Understandably, I was disappointed with my performance. Just as I was beginning to understand how to chip and putt, my biggest obstacle to success became the gray matter between my right and left ear. My fragile golf psyche negated my improved golf technique.

Jonathan, as usual, was upbeat and forward-looking. He emphasized how early I am in the learning process and how tenacious old thoughts and habits can be. "Keep on doing what you are doing. Before too long, you'll be shooting in the eighties."

At that particular moment, I was ambivalent. My attitude was identical to the guy in the New Testament who said to Jesus, "I believe. Please help my unbelief." I was assailed by self-doubt.

Just when I needed a lift, the next statement by Jonathan boosted my spirits. "You can go ahead and play some rounds of golf now," he said. "Don't worry too much about your score. Pay attention to how often you strike the ball the proper way, the way we have learned over the past three weeks."

I considered it a good sign that Jonathan was setting me loose on the course so early. I had always preferred playing to practicing. Although I would now have to split my time between the two, I was happy to have the option of a round of golf again. Jonathan's permission to play, just a small gesture of goodwill, had a big effect on my overall outlook. Sometimes, little things mean a lot.

＊＊＊＊＊＊＊＊＊＊＊＊＊＊＊

As Jonathan has remolded my swing, I have been surprised at how small each change has been. The hands-first move, though unnatural to me, involves moving my hand position just a little relative to the past. My new grip may feel uncomfortable, but my left hand has actually rotated a small distance. My butt sticks out more, but just a little more. And when Jonathan moved my arms next to my chest and I experienced that penguin-like restriction, my upper limbs had actually moved inward only three to four inches.

Remember Adam, the tall scratch golfer who gave me some pointers before lesson one? While I was doing the chipping-putting drill today, he came over to watch. He noticed how inconsistent I was and offered a few suggestions. "Above all," he said, "the second to the top button on your shirt should not move during the chip." To make his point, he showed me two photos he had taken while I was chipping today. One was of my impact position on a good chip, the other of impact during a bad chip. The main difference between the two photos was the position of that shirt button. On the good chip, it had not moved. On the bad chip, it had moved forward toward the target. Can you guess how much forward my button moved to produce that bad shot? The answer: one inch.

With golf physics, as with golf psychology, small things can make a world of difference.

Chapter 10: The Full Swing - Part II (Lesson 4)

The day after my third lesson, Cathy and I traveled to Madison, Mississippi to visit our youngest daughter. We drove there in our VW Beetle, which is great on gas mileage but low on storage space. My golf bag and clubs would not fit in the trunk, so I took just six clubs with me: driver, 5-wood, 4-iron, 7-iron, pitching wedge, and putter.

That I included the wedge, my thorn in the flesh, may seem strange, but I had noble reasons. Jesus said, "Love your enemies." Taking my pitching wedge on a vacation to Mississippi was obedience to his command. By the time we returned home four days later, another quote of Christ would seem more appropriate for that club: "Depart from me. I never knew you."

Madison is an upscale town ten miles north of Jackson. Anandale Golf Club, the home of an annual PGA tour event, is located here. Playing this private course wasn't possible, so I made other plans. Just up the road is Whisper Lake Country Club, a par-64 executive layout with two par fives, ten par threes, and six par fours. I had played this course on a previous trip and enjoyed the well-manicured grounds and friendly staff. I found it not as difficult as my home course, Cherokee Ridge, about as easy (slope 106) as Chesley Oaks, our FedUp Cup venue.

I looked forward to playing Whisper Lake again for another reason than the course itself. This would be my first round of golf since the Shoal Creek Massacre, my first in four weeks. Although I knew it was too early to assess my new swing, I wanted to see how it would hold up during a round of golf.

All in all, it held up pretty well. I shot 83, one stroke over bogey golf, which would equate to a 91 on a par-72 layout. This was acceptable, especially when taking into account that I played with only 2 woods, 3 irons, and a putter. The grades I gave my game this day are as follows:

Driver: B
5-wood: B minus
4-iron: B minus
7-iron: B plus
Wedge: C minus
Putter: C minus

On the negative side, these grades reveal that my game really hasn't changed a lot since my lessons began. In particular, I am still woefully substandard around and on the green. Fortunately, this report card does not tell the whole story. The good news today is that I hit my clubs 10-20 yards farther than ever before.

****

Lesson four with Jonathan took place two days after I returned to Alabama. We met at the driving range of Chesley Oaks and concentrated entirely on the full swing. I relayed to him the details of my round in Mississippi and told him I had a lot more work to do on my short game. His nonchalant reaction confirmed that I was merely stating the obvious.

For the first ten minutes, as I hit shots with my 7-iron, Jonathan emphasized what I had already learned about the full swing: new grip, athletic posture, straight left arm going back, good shoulder turn past the ball, and hands in front of the clubhead at impact.

"Now we're going to add three moves on the downswing that should help both your direction and distance. If you master these, you will soon be able to maneuver the ball left to right and right to left."

Hearing that we were going to focus on the downswing got my adrenaline rushing. Of all the parts of a swing, this was the least understood by me. I had no idea how to get the club from the top to impact. Some of my problems coming down, Jonathan told me, had been caused by flaws in my address and takeaway. With these corrected, perhaps I could finally uncover the mystery of the downswing.

Even for a gifted teacher like Jonathan, it was difficult to relay to me the three swing moves for today. It will be just as hard for me to put them into words. The first is a slight resetting of the hips toward the target just as the downswing begins. Jonathan refers to this as the "forward hitch". The second is keeping the buttons of my shirt from moving in front of the ball as the club descends toward it. This produces a slight lowering of my head. The third is to swing the club around my lowered head and out toward the target.

In a few minutes of patient coaching, Jonathan had me performing all three of these moves in a single swing. The closest thing in my past that compares with this is bowling. Just before releasing the ball toward the pins, I flex my knees and move my hips forward. As I release the ball, my torso stays back, causing my head to lower. My right arm then moves toward the target.

Another similar sequence happens if you side-toss a medicine ball or watermelon. Just before you bring the ball forward, you naturally set your hips ahead a little. As you toss it, your chest stays stationary and your head lowers as you bring your arms toward the poor soul trying to catch the heavy object.

Fortunately, these moves were easier to perform than describe. When I mastered all three in a swing, the ball carried lower and farther than I can remember. A few of my drives traveled 230 yards in the air, a far cry from the 200-210 range I was accustomed to. Of course, some mediocre and God-awful results were mixed in, but by the end of the day I was feeling something in the totality of my swing that was new and invigorating. My fear going forward, however, is that I will not be able to repeat this consistently or, worse yet, will lose it altogether.

At the end of the hour today, Jonathan and I compared schedules and chose Wednesday for next week's lesson.

"Let's meet at Cherokee Ridge and play some holes together. I need to watch you on the course and give you a few pointers about scoring strategy."

****

Before we move ahead, I need to address a question I promised to answer a few chapters ago. How much improvement must I make by next July to keep me playing this game?

In review, before my recent June slump I averaged 96 (24 over par) from the blue tees at Cherokee Ridge, strictly adhering to the rules. My average at Chesley Oaks, under the lenient FedUp Cup rules, was 87 (16 over par).

With this as the baseline, here are my scoring goals for July:

"Shoot This or Quit" = 25% better
    Cherokee Ridge: 90 (18 over par)
    Chesley Oaks: 83 (12 over par)

"Exceed My Expectations" = 50% better
    Cherokee Ridge: 84 (12 over par)
    Chesley Oaks: 79 (8 over par)

"What Golfer Is Inside Me?" = 75% better
    Cherokee Ridge: 78 (6 over par)
    Chesley Oaks: 75 (4 over par)

I really don't expect to achieve the 75% goal. I threw it in just to make you chuckle a bit. But if I don't improve my score by 25%, it will be no laughing matter. Fortunately, there is no need to panic yet. It is still early in my yearlong quest for improvement. I remain optimistic. Based on my progress to this point, I am confident that I will reach the minimum requirements and maintain my golfer status. But I must remain patient and realistic. Rome wasn't built in a day. Constructing my new swing will also take some time.

Chapter 11: How to Miss (Lesson 5)

I played nine holes with Jonathan today. Before each shot, he told me what strategy gave me the best chance of scoring well, specifically which club to select and where to aim. He thus became my brain up to the point I addressed the ball. After that, it was up to me.

On the tee of the first hole, a short downhill par four, he discussed my options. "There is water left, less trouble right, and trouble if you hit too long. You can take long out of the equation by hitting 3-wood instead of driver. Most of your misses are to the right, so aim down the left side of the fairway. This gives you more room for a mishit right."

Having received these instructions, I took my 3-wood, aimed down the left side of the fairway, and trusted my new swing. The ball stopped rolling in the right side of the fairway, 110 yards from the flag, just as Jonathan predicted.

"Let's now consider your approach shot," Jonathan continued. "There's a sand trap left of the green and a big drop-off to a lateral hazard on the right. The pin is back right, which brings the hazard into play if you go right and long. Short and left is your best miss. Take your pitching wedge. You usually hit this 100 yards max. If you do, you'll be on the green. If you don't, you'll most likely hit it short, which is an easier up-and-down. Aim to the left side of the green, which allows for your left-to-right trajectory."

Gripping the dreaded pitching wedge, I hit the ball a little fat (93 yards) but straight toward the flag. It landed short of the green, again just as Jonathan predicted.

Next he assessed my pitching options. "You can use either a pitching wedge or a less lofted club here. The pin is to the back and there's trouble long, so your best miss is short. Your pitching wedge is the club that can put you near the hole but not too long."

My pitch, predictably, was short, leaving a twelve foot putt for par.

"This putt breaks left to right," Jonathan told me. "An aggressive putt could roll off the back, so concentrate on distance control and try not to be too aggressive."

The result was a two-putt, a tap-in bogey.

"Bogey was about the worst you could do using this strategy. To score well, you have to expect that you will miss some shots and must plan your mishits so that you have a decent next shot."

This is how Jonathan approached all nine holes today. He allowed a chance for par while minimizing the risk for double bogey or higher. It was not a strategy I had used over the years, but it made sense to me. I could see how it could help me score better, perhaps even break 90.

No strategy, however, can atone for horrible putting, and this is exactly what Jonathan witnessed today. I had three three-putts and one four-putt in nine holes, a pitiful display of putting technique and mental focus. And it didn't take long for my coach to take notice.

"I see now where we are!" he remarked, after I missed a short putt on the fourth hole. His tone of voice was similar to a doctor at last making a diagnosis. It had become obvious to him that putting is the main reason I cannot break 90. If there was any doubt whatsoever, it vanished when I promptly four-putted the par-three fifth.

By the end of our nine holes together, Jonathan actually had me putting crosshanded. He said it was the best way to keep my wrists from breaking down during the stroke. Between you and me, I think the reason he asked me to make such a drastic change was to help clear my mind of the putting demons that torment me.

As for my overall performance today, my scorecard read "5-5-6-5-5-9-5-6-5" for a not-so-smooth 51. This included 23 putts, a far cry from Jonathan's goal of fifteen putts per nine holes. Meeting that putting goal would have given me a score of 43, two under bogey golf, and a chance of breaking 90 over eighteen holes.

"Let's meet next week here at the practice green," Jonathan said, as the teaching round ended. "We need to spend some time putting."

"Great!" I replied. "It can't come soon enough."

****

Now that putting has been exposed as my weakest link, I am determined to strengthen it. I have challenged myself to become a better putter, and I will not accept any shortcuts or excuses. Improvement in this area is now a mandate, not an option. It is, indeed, my surest route to scoring in the 80s. In fact, my entire golfing future may rest squarely on my performance with the putter over the next year.

My strategy going forward is simple. I will practice putting as if my game depends on it (for it does). I will learn the art and science of putting (for it is both). I will record the number of putts per round underneath my score (for they are linked). I will be patient and persistent (for improvement will come gradually). I will heed the advice of my teacher (for obvious reasons). And I will celebrate when I achieve my goal (for this is what I plan to do).

When it comes to putting, I must not miss the mark.

Chapter 12: Putting 102 (Lesson 6)

In case you are wondering how much time I am dedicating to this golfing adventure, let me give you the details. I have an hour-long lesson scheduled with Jonathan each week. (He has graciously spent up to two hours with me on some days.) I practice about three hours weekly at the range or putting green. And now that I have been given the go-ahead to play, I am trying to work in eighteen holes between lessons. I would like to do more, of course, but I am still full-time at the hospital and am coordinating the building of a medical clinic in Guatemala. These two obligations take priority over golf. Thus far, however, I have been able to juggle all three.

In one respect, I am glad that I must limit my golfing activities to a few hours per week. This should help ordinary golfing folk relate to my odyssey. If this journal can assist any group, it is probably those whose games are lousy, like mine, but who have yet to seek help from a professional. Such bad golfers are legion, but only a few are able and willing to seek help. Most can dedicate only a few hours each week to instruction, practice, and play. If I can succeed with this level of commitment, perhaps others may choose to take a similar path toward improvement.

****

I played my round of golf this week at my home course, Cherokee Ridge. Cathy, my wife and biggest fan, rode along with me. I shot 48 on the front nine and 47 on the back. I did not play quite as well from tee to green as I did in Mississippi, in part because the Ridge is much tighter and has a lower margin for error. My putting and chipping were better but still inconsistent.

The score of 95 probably means the June slump is over. Thanks to Jonathan, my scoring resembles what it was at the start of the year. The difference between now and then is that I have a consistent plan of action directed by someone in the know, not a helter-skelter string of best guesses orchestrated by me. My 95 this week was the most productive and least stressful of any above-bogey round I have ever played. For the first time in my life, I am learning as I play.

****

Lesson six took place at the putting green of Cherokee Ridge. Last week's round together put "teach the good doctor how to putt" at the top of Jonathan's "to do" list. To decrease my putts per round from over forty to near thirty is going to take all the innate skill he possesses as a teacher. He is aware of the challenge, but he also knows that the stakes are high and worth the effort. I could tell by his focus and his tone of voice as he instructed today.

"Putt these balls toward that hole," he said, pointing to a cup thirty feet away.

After I had putted a few times, Jonathan proceeded to step 2. "When you hit the next putt toward the hole, don't look where it goes. Then I'm going to drop a second ball, and I want you to putt it toward the same hole. Your job is to tell me if you think the second ball traveled shorter or longer than the first."

For the next few minutes, I alternated between putt #1 and putt #2. For the most part, I was able to correctly judge which had traveled farther just by the feel of the two putts.

After a couple of variations to this drill, Jonathan finally revealed the reason for this odd exercise. "You are a feel putter, just like I am. You roll the ball better if you try to imagine the whole putt. Others perform better if they aim at a point on the line instead of sensing the whole putt."

"What good does it do to know I'm a feel putter?" I asked.

"It helps you understand how to approach a putt before you actually hit the ball. You should concentrate on the line of the putt in general and feel the putt backward from the hole to you. Then you should address the ball and strike it along that line back to the hole. That's how feel putters should approach putting."

The remainder of our time together today was spent doing just that. I practiced the art of "feeling" putts of various lengths and breaks. In addition, Jonathan emphasized a few technical points:

1. He stressed the importance of a pre-putt routine that never wavers. From now on, I will first visualize the putt while standing behind the ball. Next I will assume my putting stance and take a practice stroke along that line. Only then will I place the head of my putter behind the ball, visualize the line once more, and strike the putt.

Jonathan warned again and again that I should never deviate from this pre-shot routine.

2. He again stressed the importance of keeping the second button of my shirt stationary during the entire putting stroke.

3. He stressed the importance of keeping my head down during the stroke, not looking up too soon.

4. He added a pendulum motion of my left shoulder, rocking downward during the take-away and upward during the forward stroke.

5. He stressed the importance of centering the ball on the putterface with each stroke. He referred me to a line on the top of my putterhead that marks its sweet spot. I had never before tried to place this line directly behind the ball. After today, I always will.

Jonathan ended the lesson by repeating my goal of thirty putts per round. This, I fear, may be a bit ambitious. I read in a book this week that the touring pros average 27.5 to 30.5 putts per round and that thirty-two putts is a good goal for amateurs. Regardless, the truth remains that it will be hard for me to break 90 consistently with forty-plus putts in eighteen holes. My putting must get better as I approach the fork in the cart path ahead. Thankfully, Jonathan today gave me the blueprint for improvement. Now it is up to me to make that plan a reality.

****

By the time Jonathan and I meet for lesson seven, my family and I will have spent a week's vacation in Destin, Florida. Hopefully, I will have practiced or played golf almost every day. I will know a lot more about the state of my game, especially my putting. Will I break 90 at least once? Will my number of putts per round dip into the mid-thirties? Will my pitching wedge and I finally be on speaking terms when I return home?

I will share these answers with Jonathan next week.

Chapter 13: Why I Miss (Lesson 7)

Between lessons six and seven, I enjoyed a week's vacation and played three rounds of golf. The first was at Gunter's Landing Golf Course in Guntersville, Alabama. It is a beautiful layout near Guntersville Lake and is widely regarded as the most difficult golfing venue in Marshall County. Its course rating (71.2) and slope (134) from the blue tees (6419 yards) are higher than Cherokee Ridge (70.7 and 129 at 6439 yards). In my opinion, this under-estimates the difference between the two. I have always found Gunter's Landing to be a challenge from start to finish.

My front-nine score of 51 was about as ugly as it sounds. My new swing wasn't clicking, my new putting style wasn't working, and my new course strategy wasn't reducing strokes. I was a bit discouraged as I made the turn, but I continued the new swing and resisted the temptation to revert to the old. I was rewarded by the gods of golf with a 43 on the back nine, which included some of the longest drives and best approach shots of my life. Had my chipping and putting not failed me on several holes, the score would have been lower. I had 41 total putts, which is not even close to my goal. The undulating greens and difficult pin placements were partly responsible, but once again I must take most of the blame. Nevertheless, a below-bogey back nine at Gunter's Landing was a step in the right direction.

The other two rounds were played at Kelly Plantation Golf Club in Destin, Florida. This Freddie Couples signature course is one of the most beautiful pieces of golf real estate I have seen. It, too, is difficult for aspiring bogey golfers like me. I played the green tees (6521 yards) on both days. The course rating of 71.8 and slope of 136 were even higher than Gunter's Landing. Aware of the challenge before me, I spent two hours the day before at the practice facility focusing on chipping and putting, trying to ingrain what Jonathan has been teaching.

The first round there was frustrating, to say the least. I played with my two sons-in-law, who have seldom struck a golf ball the past twelve months due to work and family obligations. Our scores were 102 (Randy), 102 (Scott), and 103 (Alan), a sad commentary on a father-in-law who has played at least fifteen rounds of golf and taken six lessons in the past three months. I sprayed the ball everywhere from tee to green and chipped like a novice. My only salvation was my putting. Thirty-seven putts in eighteen holes was a little better than my recent performances. All in all, my 54-48 was a downer, a setback on my journey toward improvement.

Day 2 at Kelly Plantation started the same. I played by myself and after only seven holes was thirteen over par. My drives and approach shots were going right and left into hazards, and penalty strokes were accumulating faster than the sweat beads on my skin. Ironically, my chipping and putting improved on this day, just as my accuracy from tee to green declined. My golf game was becoming similar to a blanket that I pulled over my head, only to uncover my feet. Compounding my problems, distance with my clubs was not as good as it had been at Gunter's Landing. Something was amiss with my new swing. I was not obeying a rule Jonathan had laid down for me. I just couldn't figure out what it was.

On the eighth tee, a 170-yard par three, I mumbled aloud, "I just can't hit it as far today. I might as well quit trying." I decided to adjust my projected distance with each club downward by 10-15 yards and to concentrate on a smoother swing. After a par and bogey on holes eight and nine, I continued this approach on the back nine. The result was a score of 44 that actually was better than it sounds. For the first time in a long while, every club in my bag, even the pitching wedge, contributed positively. I had only eighteen putts, got up-and-down on three holes (including once from the sand), and had better control of distance and direction on drives and approach shots. My score of 94 (50-44) was eight strokes better than the day before. The last eleven holes, in particular, seemed far removed from my dismal performance during the Shoal Creek Massacre.

So what is my overall assessment of my golf game after playing these three rounds? If I take the best nine holes each day (43, 48, 44), the average is 45, right at bogey golf. For one-half of my rounds, therefore, I am on the cusp of scoring in the 80s. I realize someone could accuse me of manipulating the numbers so that it appears I am improving. Be assured, I am not wearing blinders. As a physician, I know that diabetic control cannot be measured by considering only the best blood glucose readings. The higher values must also be taken into account. In the same way, I cannot boast about breaking 90 for eighteen holes when the average of my worst nine holes is over 50. What I can claim, however, is that I am now able to play under-bogey golf for a long stretch each round. If I can extend this string of good golf a few more holes, a score in the 80s is in sight.

Am I close to such a breakthrough? Or am I still too inconsistent to reach my goal? I am not sure which is true, but I do know this: I'm not there yet and have much work ahead of me.

****

Back at Chesley Oaks, lesson seven was split between putting and the full swing. Jonathan first gave me some pointers in reading greens. He convinced me that plumb-bobbing (holding the putter in front of me to determine the line) was not as accurate as I thought it was. Instead, he encouraged me to examine the contour of the green from all sides of the hole. I was worried this would turn me into a slow player, but he assured me it would not take much time. He was right. A quick look at the putt from all directions did not seem time-consuming and did help me read a putt more accurately.

Jonathan next had me concentrate on the speed of my takeaway and follow-through with my putts. He wanted me to be a little quicker with my stroke. He said it would help me keep the ball on my intended line. He also had me focus on the length of my putting stroke. My tendency on long putts, he said, is for my takeaway to be too long and my follow-through too short. This leads to a push: the ball travels right of where I am aiming. On short putts, the opposite occurs: my takeaway is too short and my follow-though too long, leading to a leftward pull. By focusing on a symmetric stroke, I instantly corrected these faults.

What Jonathan did today with my putting was revolutionary to me. In the past, I knew when I mishit a putt and whether it was a push or pull, but I never knew why it happened. Now I can diagnose and treat many of my putting problems merely by observing where I miss. Such awareness is invaluable if a golfer truly wants to learn as he plays.

When we finished putting and moved to the driving range, I gave Jonathan a summary of my three rounds during vacation.

"I knew my distance was off and my trajectory was too high," I explained to him, "but I couldn't figure out what I was doing wrong."

Jonathan continued with the "why you miss" theme.

"Hit a few balls with your 7-iron and let me see what your swing looks like."

In less than five minutes, he told me what I was doing wrong and how to correct it, and my distance and ball flight were immediately restored.

"When you are not swinging well, you can tell by your distance and ball flight what you are doing wrong. Let me give you some things to remember."

Just like he did with my putting, Jonathan then told me why my shots go astray.

"If you hit it high and short, like you did on vacation, your left elbow is probably breaking down on the backswing, leading to wrist-flipping at impact. Keep that elbow straight and your ball will go lower and farther."

"If you are hitting it left, concentrate on your upper body. Make sure the button of your shirt is stationary during the downswing and at impact. If it moves forward, your misses will tend to be left."

"If you are hitting it right, concentrate on your hips and shoulders during the backswing. Your hips should rotate just a little and your shoulders a lot as you take the club back. If you over-rotate your hips and under-rotate your shoulders, you will tend to misfire to the right."

Jonathan summarized: "Hit your shot. Diagnose your miss. Correct your swing. That's what you should do from now on."

And that is exactly what we did the remainder of today's lesson.

****

As we walked to our vehicles after the lesson, I mustered the courage to ask Jonathan how I was doing after seven sessions.

"As far as your swing is concerned, you are ahead of schedule. I have been surprised how quickly you have mastered the swing changes I have asked you to make. But you are behind schedule when it comes to your scoring. The way you are hitting the ball, you should be shooting in the high 80s. It all comes down to your short game and putting. Improve these and your scoring will catch up with your swing."

As I drove away in my car, I thought about Jonathan's assessment. Having a pretty swing is great and wonderful, but that is not my goal. Improved scoring —breaking 90 at Cherokee Ridge and 85 at Chesley Oaks—is how I will gauge success or failure. Hopefully, a better swing will soon lead to a lower score. If not, it is all for naught. What do you call a fisherman who casts his line perfectly all day but catches no fish? The answer: a failure. So it is with golf. At the end of the day, pretty doesn't matter. Only the number on the scorecard does.

Chapter 14: Psychotherapy (Lesson 8)

On Wednesday of this week, I played a morning round of golf prior to my eighth lesson. My playing partners were Barry and Charlie, two of our FedUp Cup participants. The course was Cherokee Ridge. The tees were the whites (shorter than what I usually play), and the format was FedUp (highest score possible was a double bogey).

Barry and Charlie are better golfers than I am, usually scoring 5-10 strokes lower per eighteen holes. They are representative of where I want my game to be at the end of my year of lessons. I think this is why I felt more nervous than usual as I stood on the first tee. I knew this round would be a barometer of where I am and how far I have to go.

Judging from my performance, I have many miles to travel. I shot a 91, which at first glance doesn't seem so bad, until you consider that I was playing from easier tees and that I picked up my ball after a double bogey. Barry and Charlie shot 83 and 85, respectively. Charlie won four holes outright. Barry won three holes. I won none.

More troubling than the score itself was the way I played overall. I drove the ball okay, as usual, and placed myself in position to win several holes, but I always wilted under the pressure and hit a lousy shot. To put it bluntly, I choked more than a hard-to-start lawn mower. My nerves got the best of me, and the result at the end of the day was the same as always. I finished last, 5-10 strokes behind Barry and Charlie.

When I met Jonathan afterwards for my lesson, I was in need of a pep talk. I was down on myself, frustrated by my lack of composure under pressure. If Jonathan was a football coach, I would have accepted extra laps as punishment well deserved. Since he was a golf coach, I didn't know how he would deal with my bad play.

"The mental side of golf is a beast sometimes," Jonathan began, after I summarized the round I just finished. "Ask Tiger Woods. Ask David Duval. Ask me."

Since Tiger and David were not present, I asked Jonathan about his struggles with the mind, especially those pressure-packed moments golf has thrown his way.

"I remember playing in a Tennessee vs. Georgia professional tournament with a Ryder Cup format. I was paired with and competing against golfers who had made it to Q-school the previous year, one step from the PGA. On the first hole we drew to see who would tee off first, and the lot fell to me. With all eyes gazing in my direction, I hooked my drive into a nearby tree. It came to a stop on the ladies' tee."

"Ouch!" I said, imagining how embarrassed he must have felt. "What did you do next?"

"I figured the worst was over, so I relaxed. I hit the next shot short of the green, pitched it close, and sank the putt for a par. I played well the rest of the round, and my partner and I won our match."

"So what is your secret for performing well under pressure?" I asked.

"First, you must believe in your swing, even when pressure makes you doubt. Believe in what you've practiced. Believe in what has worked under less pressure."

I was having a hard time relating to this first step. "What about people like me who have no reason to trust their swing and no history of consistency to lean on?"

"That will come with time and practice," he replied. "Until then, you must trust what you have learned and try not to get too rigid on pressure shots. Concentrate on being smooth and fluid, and your results will improve."

The rest of the lesson was spent practicing smoothness under pressure. Jonathan challenged me to a short game contest and invited Chris, a regular golfer at our club, to compete against me. My task was to chip the ball exactly as I had learned and to concentrate on a fluid stroke. As I did this, I noticed improved results, much better than what had transpired earlier during my round. Several times I chipped it closer than Chris.

"It's all about trust," Jonathan repeated. "Trust what you have been taught. Make sure you have a smooth motion when pressure mounts. And one thing more: don't overreact if the shot goes astray. Having confidence and a fluid swing won't work every time, but I guarantee this approach will save the day more than any other."

Jonathan didn't do a lot of tweaking of my swing during this lesson. He sensed I needed a psychiatrist more than a technician after my frustrating round. The only take-home tip he gave me was to lengthen my follow-through on my chips. This helped keep my stroke less rigid and jerky, and it also improved my direction. I believe this longer follow-through will help my short game, especially during pressure situations.

The following day, Jonathan sent me this text:

I wanted to give you a thought from yesterday. As I thought about what we did and talked about, I don't know if the point was clear. You are reaching the point now when improvement will be on a smaller scale. Sometimes the improvement will not be measurable in score but in awareness.

The main thoughts from yesterday should be:

1. *technical - fluid motion trumps rigid/tight, especially in times of pressure to perform;*
2. *mental - golf score management is a process of recognized chaos control (what am I feeling before, during, and after the shot at hand and how do I respond?).*

You are at the point where learning to trust what you have trained your body to do in the golf swing has to be constantly reinforced. Do not doubt what you are trying to do. The failure rate in golf is high. We fail to hit shots on line and the correct distance almost 98% of the time; otherwise, we would knock every shot in from the fairway! Celebrate the wins no matter how small and forget the losses instantly.

Hope this helps add some clarity.

That weekend, Jonathan played in a tournament in Dothan, Alabama. It was his first competitive round in over a year. He texted me that he didn't hit the ball well the first day but did manage to scratch and claw his way around the course, relying heavily on his short game. I didn't have to ask him if his chips and putts were fluid. His score of 74 told me everything I needed to know.

As for me, I have not yet developed Jonathan's grace under fire. Perhaps I never will. There are some people, like basketball star Charles Barkley, who cannot silence the demons that torment them when a golf ball is addressed. Could I be in the same league? Right now, thankfully, I am not as possessed as Barkley, but I am nowhere near the mindset of Jonathan and still a few steps behind Barry and Charlie.

When I wrote in an earlier chapter that I hoped Jonathan was an exorcist, you probably thought I was kidding. I wasn't. Please continue to approach me on the golf course with caution. I remain a bit unstable.

Chapter 15: A Better Approach (Lesson 9)

I came to my ninth lesson armed with a list of statistics. Little did I know that Jonathan was loaded with stats as well.

My numbers were an overview of the two rounds of golf I had played at Cherokee Ridge since we last met. There was some good news: 92 and 91 from the blues with strict scoring, 33 and 35 putts per eighteen holes, and a much improved short game. But there was one negative statistic that offset the good, a trend that has to change soon: my poor percentage of greens hit in regulation.

To land a ball on the green in regulation, I need to hit a good drive and a good approach shot. (On par fives, of course, there is a lay-up shot between the two.) When it comes to driving, I am doing okay. Of the twenty-eight holes that were par fours and fives, I was in a good position to reach the green in regulation seventeen times. My performance on approach shots, however, left a lot to be desired. I was on the green in regulation on just three holes. On the other fourteen approach shots, I ended up off the green with something other than a putter in my hand for my next shot.

Such a horrible GIR percentage makes breaking 90 regularly almost impossible, for a couple of reasons. First, it basically eliminates birdie from the equation during my rounds. Second, it puts pressure on my short game, my weakest link, to save par or salvage a bogey. This is why my percentage of successful approach shots must improve if I am to reach my goal of under-bogey golf.

During the two best rounds I have ever played in my life, I remember hitting a much larger number of greens than usual. This now has to become the norm.

I still agree with Jonathan that improving my short game, not the approach shot, is the surest way to lower my score. I heard Monday on the Golf Channel that the PGA pros hit only 65% of greens in regulation during last week's tournament. This means they averaged missing the green six times a round. They made up for this with their short game (pitching, chipping, bunker shots, and putting). Likewise, my short game will also make or break me on my journey. But I am just as convinced that my GIR percentage of 22% must also improve if I am to reach my goal. I am now aiming for six greens (33%) hit in regulation during future rounds.

My question to Jonathan at the start of today's lesson was, "How can I accomplish this?" He promptly pulled some papers from his golf bag and shared with me some tour statistics that helped answer my question. His information was a comparison of Rory McIroy, the world's #1, with the player ranked 125. The biggest statistical difference between the two was Rory's percentage of putts made from eight feet in. But something else was obvious as we reviewed the numbers, a fact that could help solve the riddle of the approach shot. Each player, it appeared, had a favorite yardage and a not-so-favorite yardage on approaches. Rory's largest percentage of GIR was from 100 yards and his lowest was from 175 yards. Player #125 preferred to be 125 yards away on approach shots but did not like to be 75 yards out.

Jonathan interpreted the stats for me. "To hit more greens, we first have to find your best yardage and your worst yardage. Then we need to play each hole striving to create approach shots near your favorite distances and to avoid your worst distances."

Jonathan then had me hit balls to different targets to determine my go-to range. The results were not surprising to me. I was worst from 100-120 yards, better from 120-140 yards and from 160-180 yards, and best from 140-160 yards.

"You need to play each hole trying to achieve a 130-170 yard approach shot. That is your confidence distance. You won't be able to do this every time, but you'll get close more times than not. The end result will be more greens in regulation."

Jonathan's next task was to discover my ideal ball flight. He had me hit several more shots, trying to see if I should play a draw or a fade. His conclusion was that the fade is my preferred ball flight, the one I can control more often.

"With golf," he explained, "you don't have to control everything. But you do have to control something."

He then shared three things I need to do to land more approach shots on the green:

(1) Try to keep my distance at 130-170 yards.
(2) Try to hit a fade.
(3) Always visualize the shot beforehand.

The rest of the lesson was spent trying to do those three things. Jonathan helped me develop a pre-shot routine that included visualization of the ball flight. He gave me a few hints on hitting a fade. He put a 7-iron, 6-iron, 5-iron, 4-iron, and 3-iron in my hand, the clubs I use from 130-170 yards. Lastly, he gave me strict orders to use this strategy on the course.

****

Things have changed a lot since early July. After nine lessons, I now have a consistent pre-shot routine, a more athletic set-up, a revamped full swing, a preferred ball flight, a go-to approach distance, an improved chipping stroke, a different putting style, and a common-sense course strategy.

Scoring, however, is the same old story. I'm still stuck in the 90s. My task from this day forward is to use the foundation above to improve golf's most important statistic: strokes per round.

Chapter 16: First Quarter Report
(Lessons 10 and 11)

As I write these words, it is September 25. Summer has officially given way to fall, and I am now three months into my journey toward better golf. At the end of this month, I will be one-fourth of the way to July, to that pivotal fork in the cart path. I think it's a good time to pause and gauge where I am.

I have listed below the scores from my last four rounds at Cherokee Ridge. All were from the blue tees under strict rules. In case you have forgotten, I averaged 96 from these tees one year ago and over 100 during my recent June swoon. To continue to play golf next July, I must be able to maintain an average score of 90 from the same blue tees.

The following reveals how far I've come and how far I have to go. It also indicates what parts of my game need the most work:

SCORING	91	(44-47)
	95	(46-49)
	93	(47-46)
	95	(49-46)
	average: 93.5	(46.5-47.0)

BIRDIES:	0-0-0-0	
PARS:	5-4-5-5	average: 4.75
BOGEYS:	8-7-9-6	average: 7.5
DOUBLES:	4-6-1-4	average: 3.75

TRIPLES: 1-0-2-3   average: 1.5
PENGUINS: 0-1-1-0   average: 0.5

GREENS IN REGULATION: 3-2-3-1   average: 2.25

NEAR-GIR (<50 yards from flag): 7-8-10-9
average: 8.5

UP AND DOWN FROM <50YARDS
    4 of 11   2 of 12
    3 of 12   3 of 13   average: 3 of 12

PUTTS: 34-32-35-33   average 33.5

What do these stats tell me? An honest self-appraisal yields the following points:

1. My putting is much better.
2. My scoring is almost three strokes better than a year ago and at least eight strokes better than the day of my first lesson in July.
3. I am on the green or near the green in regulation about 60% of the time, short of my goal of 75%. Therefore, my performance from tee to green needs to improve.
4. On the average, I record a par or bogey on twelve holes per round. Six holes, therefore, are "come apart" experiences. Somehow I must reduce the number of high scores on my card.
5. Although my pitching and chipping are better, they have not improved to the point that it shows in the stats. My percentage of up-and-downs from less than 50 yards remains poor. Improvement here seems to be the quickest path to scoring

consistently in the 80s, something Jonathan has been saying all along.

As for Jonathan, no one knows where I stand better than he does. He actually accompanied me on one of the rounds above and thus experienced firsthand the state of my game. For a good golfer and excellent teacher like him, it must have been painful to watch. In the future, I have offered to medicate him prior to a round together to minimize his emotional trauma.

During the timeframe of the four rounds above, I had two lessons. Jonathan and I worked on my full swing, trying to create a reproducible stroke, one I can always depend on, one that will yield consistent results. To be more specific, he is trying to get me to hit the ball on a gentle left to right trajectory (i.e. a soft fade). He is also encouraging me to remain positive and upbeat on the course, to always expect good results, to truly be surprised and shocked when the ball goes astray. What's more, he wants me to concentrate during every shot on his five "core knowledge points": (1) hands in front of the clubface at impact; (2) level shoulder rotation with straight left arm; (3) stable head and shirt button; (4) pause at the top; (5) lower body "forward hitch" to start the downswing. I also must remember to select the right club, take the proper grip, follow my pre-shot routine, assume an athletic posture, and drive my right shoulder toward the target, somehow managing to maintain my balance at all times.

These are difficult assignments, to say the least, and I do not think I am faring very well. First of all, my ball trajectory is most often right to left, just the opposite of a fade. Secondly, I am anything but positive on the golf course. In order to be confident before each shot, I must constantly lie to myself about how shaky my game is. This may be easy for some people, but I am having a hard time repetitively and intentionally deceiving myself. (If Pinocchio did what Jonathan is asking me to do, he would soon be able to putt with his nose.) And thirdly, when it comes to balance during my swing, I look eerily similar to an on-the-street Weather Channel reporter during a hurricane.

The honeymoon with my new swing is now over. For the first time since my lessons started, I am getting a bit frustrated with myself about my lack of progress. And I am beginning to have sincere doubts whether or not I will ever achieve my goal. I told Jonathan at my last lesson that I am his Charles Barkley, a golf teacher's worst nightmare. No matter how hard I try to change my habits, there's a little bad golfer inside me that refuses to let go of the past. Despite Jonathan's valiant efforts, it seems like I am taking two steps forward then a couple of steps back, going absolutely nowhere.

I don't blame Jonathan in any way. It's not his fault that I feel like a hamster on a treadmill. I alone am responsible for my present woes. He is doing a great job playing the part of Moses, doing everything he can to lead me out of golfing bondage. I, on the other hand, have not responded appropriately to his instruction. I have yet to truly follow his lead. If the children of Israel were like me, they never would have seen the parting of the Red Sea. They would have remained enslaved in Egypt. They never would have reached the Promised Land.

If things don't change, neither will I.

Chapter 17: Moving Forward
(Lessons 12 and 13)

Today there is much rejoicing in heaven, and I'm pretty ecstatic myself here on earth. A miracle just as jaw-dropping as the parting of the Red Sea has occurred. Something has happened that is as mathematically unlikely as feeding five thousand people with five loaves and two fish. In world history, it's the biggest upset since David slew Goliath, a feat greater than making an axehead float or turning water into wine. And it has happened to someone as undeserving as Saul on the Damascus Road.

Move over, Elijah. Step aside for a minute, Moses. Making water burn like gasoline and turning a stick into a snake are not as impressive as what happened in Marshall County, Alabama this week.

Randy Stewart broke 90 at Cherokee Ridge!

Yes, when I gazed into the mirror this morning, I was staring at a man who just carded a smooth 87 from the blue tees under rules as strict as the pros on the PGA Tour.

The event has literally transformed my inner golfing self. As the Beatles sang, "I'm not half the man I used to be." A good golfer has moved into my body and taken residence next to the bad golfer who has lived alone there for four decades. And now, just like the Israelites after forty years of wilderness wandering, the Promised Land has come into view.

Want to know more about my round? I thought you'd never ask! I recorded five pars, a birdie, two bogeys, and one double bogey on the front nine for a 39, then came back to earth on the back with a 48. What was most encouraging was the fact that the low scores were not flukes. There were no miracle shots, just sound ball striking from tee to green, a good short game, and decent putting. On this October day, at least, I was a much better golfer than any time in my past and light-years removed from June of this year. The emotion I experienced as I walked off the eighteenth green was similar to what a butterfly must feel when it emerges from the cocoon. I finally had my golfing wings.

Before you remind me that it's only one round, let me assure you that I have not lost sight of the bigger picture. A single score below 90 doesn't mark the successful end of my journey. I must consistently shoot this number or lower to continue as a golfer next July. But it is also true that the first step to breaking 90 consistently is to do it the first time. That's why I am so excited. I am like the frustrated nerd, longing to get married, who finally is able to get a date. It doesn't guarantee matrimony, but it's a good first step. After my 87 this week, I am now walking hand in hand in with my clubs in golfing nerd-dom.

This turnaround was quick and unexpected. Just last week I was assailed by self-doubt, wondering if I would ever make it. I was down on myself, and I was afraid that I was failing my teacher, too. How, then, do I explain the sudden improvement? The answer can be found in my last two lessons, when Jonathan asked me to do something new on the downswing. It was a tip that changed everything.

During my first eleven lessons, Jonathan had methodically tweaked every part of my full swing. My pre-shot routine was different. So were my set-up, takeaway, impact position, and follow-through. But, in my opinion, there was something else I needed to be doing, a missing link that would complete my swing. I didn't know what was lacking but was convinced it had something to do with the downswing, for years the most mysterious move in golf. I was equally convinced that I would never get beyond my present doldrums until I learned and mastered this hidden nugget.

During lessons twelve and thirteen, Jonathan helped me put this piece of the puzzle in place. I will not bore you with the technical details—again, this is not meant to be an instructional book—but will summarize the missing link as a movement of my body forward toward the target as the club descends to the ball. Without telling me how to do it, Jonathan simply asked me to keep everything I had learned the same and then move my lower body toward the target as I attempted to hit the ball. Instantly, the contact was crisper, the ball flight straighter, the outcome better. By moving forward on the downswing, my game leap-frogged ahead as well.

"This is when golf becomes fun," Jonathan told me, as lesson thirteen ended. He was right. My very next round was that 87 at Cherokee Ridge. I haven't enjoyed golf so much in a long, long time.

The challenge before me now is to build on this foundation. I must continue to spend the necessary time on the practice range, putting green, and golf course. I must faithfully execute the various parts of the swing that Jonathan has shown to me. Above all, I must not lose perspective. I will celebrate this milestone but must also treat it as a signpost leading to the destination, not the destination itself. In other words, I must continually remind myself that I have not yet arrived.

Golf, more than any other sport, is a fragile game, and we golfers tend to be fragile creatures. Today's successes are not guarantees for tomorrow. Nothing can be assumed or taken for granted. A golfer who rests on his laurels because he has "found it" will soon find himself lost. Unless he continues in discovery mode, he will realize how fleeting success can be. He must always be learning, striving to take his game to another level. An aspiring golfer like me, therefore, must never waver in his determination. The surest path to success is to never detour from a successful path.

In this respect, trying to improve in golf is similar to trying to lose weight. If you don't stay with it, you won't succeed. Yo-yo dieters remain obese because they stop trying to lose. At best, they remain the same over time. More often than not, they gradually get fatter. After successfully shedding ten pounds the past year and managing to keep them off, I have come to the conclusion that the only way to maintain my weight is to continue to stick to my diet and my exercise routine. In weight loss, as in golf, the quickest route to failure is to quit trying to succeed.

This would be the perfect time to share ten similarities between losing weight and dropping strokes:

1. It is easy to add pounds to your waist but hard to take them off. Likewise, it's easier to gain strokes on your scorecard than to lose them.

2. Concentrating on the short game (what you do near the refrigerator and around the green) is the quickest route to success.
3. It's easy to spot a bad dieter and a bad golfer. Mirrors and scales don't lie; neither do swings and scorecards.
4. Advice abounds for the overweight and the over-par, and people with good figures and low scores are quick to give it.
5. A steady diet of fowl (chicken and turkey) sheds pounds. A steady diet of fowl (birdies and eagles) sheds strokes.
6. Weight loss, like golf, is a relative activity. There is usually a relative more overweight and over-par than you are.
7. God loves both the hefty and the hacker and has provided a way of escape (Jenny Craig and Jonathan Lynch).
8. Gaining and golfing can be done in community (with your family or foursome) or in isolation (on the couch or at the range).
9. To succeed, golfers must stop slicing and hooking their drives. Likewise, the obese must stop slicing and hooking their desserts.
10. Losing five pounds in one week does not make you a slim person. Shedding five strokes in one round does make you a good golfer.

So onward I go! Like the apostle Paul, who had not yet attained his goal, I will press on toward mine. Like a baby butterfly emerging from the cocoon, I will attempt to soar to heights I've never seen. Like the 500-pounder on television who weighs 350 at mid-season, I will double my efforts to be the one who loses the most strokes at year's end.

Before I do, however, would you allow me to take a victory lap? The Israelites marching around Jericho stopped long enough to blow their horns. May I stop long enough to blow mine?

Extra, extra! Read all about it!
Randy Stewart Broke 90 This Week
And walls of doubt came tumbling down.

Chapter 18: Perspective

The middle of October brought a hiatus from golf, as I joined eleven other Marshall County residents for a week of medical missions in Jalapa, Guatemala. It was my fifth trip to this poor area, where a clinic is being built that will provide ongoing medical care. My first visit in 2011 was a life-changing experience, and each subsequent trip has reinforced my resolve to partner with the church there to offer medical and spiritual assistance to the poorest of the poor.

Golf is nowhere on Jalapa's radar. In five weeks there over four years, I have never seen a club or a ball, have never viewed a golf advertisement in video or print, and have yet to hear one word from a Guatemalan about golf in general. While there, golf is not on my radar either. I never think about the game or my swing or my next round. In fact, if someone tried to strike up a conversation with me about golf, I would change the subject. Things more essential and basic are in play. The need there transcends any sporting activity.

To help you understand why I feel so strongly about this area and its people, I will share with you the testimony I gave to my church upon returning from my first trip. It sums up what is really important in life. It puts everything, golf included, in proper perspective.

November, 2011

Dear Church family,

In years past I have sat where you are sitting, listening to reports from volunteers returning from mission work. I have looked at their pictures, heard their testimonies, and marveled at their sacrifice. On every occasion, I have had a strong feeling that their mission report could not convey the deeper aspects of being on the mission field. I felt it was impossible for people, returning from a place far away, to relay to me the full meaning of their days of mission work. And I felt it was impossible for me, in Alabama during those days, to grasp the depth of their experience. It seemed to me that they were somewhat in the position of an astronaut trying to explain what it was like to walk on the moon. Words can only get the audience so far. So much, beyond words, is tied to the experience itself. You have to have been there to fully understand.

Tonight I find myself on the other side of the fence, behind the microphone instead of in the pew. And what I had suspected in years past is indeed true. There is no way I can fully convey to you how rich and deep this week has been. It is an impossible task. Nevertheless, this is the task before me. Like the returning astronaut, I will do the best that I can do.

1. The first thing I want you to realize is **how much you were with us** in Guatemala. In all, we carried over 66,000 pills; you donated 44,000 of them. We carried 150 tubes of medicine, all donated by church members. A significant percentage of our liquid meds also came from you. What's more, the purchase of the extra medication

was funded in large part by your monetary gifts. Add to this your prayers and encouragement before and during the trip and the $4500 you gave for putting a roof on the church there, and you get a sense of how much you were involved. What is so hard for me to convey to you, however, and what I had never imagined until now, is how palpable your presence was. In almost a mysterious and mystical way, it was like you were there standing with us, loving with us, crying with us, laughing with us, praying with us. You were never far from our side. As surely as God was present in Guatemala, so were you.

2. And that brings me to a second hard-to-describe aspect of this trip: **the presence of Christ in our midst** in Guatemala. The Bible says that God is near to the brokenhearted. I am now convinced that He is also near to those who minister to them. How I have neglected this in the past! I have not ministered enough to the needy, and I have been the loser. I am sure that I am not alone. Many of us spend very little of our precious time descending in love to those less fortunate; then we wonder why God does not seem present and real in our lives. We have confined our Christianity so much to the sanctuary and to our city—to people similar to us —that we have been able to touch only the periphery of the presence of God.

Hearing the testimony of our mission teams in previous years, I never appreciated how much Christ had touched them, walked with them, spoke to them, and encouraged them. I literally had no idea. And what a wonderful joy I missed! Christ has called us to follow *him*, to work at *his* side, and we will find him most often where the poor, sick, troubled, and outcast live. A journey to Guatemala is not required. People who are down-and-out are living right here in our city, county, and state. Wherever they are, Jesus is there, just as he was in Guatemala.

3. I now move to a third impossible-to-explain aspect of the past week, and it is one that I must convey to you as tenderly as possible. I never realized until now **how much we take worship for granted**. I said *we*, so that includes me, a worship leader. What is Christian worship? It is a group of people meeting together to express devotion to God, to thank Jesus for his unfailing love, and to acknowledge God's Spirit within them. In Guatemala, I saw pure worship as I have seldom seen it: people, in the most destitute circumstances imaginable, singing boldly and joyously in Spanish our great hymns —*At the Cross*, *Marching On*, and *Victory in Jesus*—with only a portable CD player to aid them. In America, I see people, blessed with prosperity and good health, singing on Sunday mornings without passion, as if the goal is to get to the next part of the service and move on. In Guatemala, I saw people, both children and adults, remaining after the invitation on a cool mountain night to hear their pastor share with new converts and to sing a parting hymn. In America, I see people, both young and old, exiting during the closing chorus because worship is *finally* over.

But is this worship at all? I am as guilty as anyone. Even as a minister of music, my worship has many times been too mechanical, too exterior, too time-constrained. I have often approached Sunday services half-heartedly. In contrast, worship there was pure and spontaneous. I never dreamed that worship could be so different from us yet so similar to us. The praise of the Guatemalan Christians was not charismatic but very "Baptist". (Not one hand was raised.) It was far from innovative. (We sang the same old melodies and text.) It did not approach the level of perfection that we are accustomed to and strive for here, but it was the most perfect worship I have ever experienced. The reason: the Guatemalans gave their whole hearts to God in praise, for there was nothing else they could give Him.

4. The final thing about this trip that is hard to convey is **the depth of need in Guatemala**. In all, we treated over nine hundred patients, ranging in age from one month to 103 years. Most of them had multiple complaints and illnesses. Everyone with abdominal pain received a medication for parasites, because parasitic disease is so prevalent in the area. The cases we encountered were sometimes overwhelming and heart-breaking: a man with a grossly disfigured face due to an abscess, who endured a painful and bloody procedure to drain the infection; several girls in their mid-teens, pregnant with their first or second child; a 16-year-old boy with left-sided blindness, unable to see an eye specialist; a young girl covered with a rough, black, hairy rash on her neck and chest, present since birth and now spreading to her legs; multiple patients with diabetes and high blood pressure, unable to afford medicine or obtain medical follow-up; a five-year-old boy with a partially developed sixth toe that we surgically removed; a 22-year-old man with repetitive seizures daily, desperately in need of medication adjustment and long-term care. You can add to the nine hundred we treated thousands of others in Guatemala who are likewise afflicted. In and around Jalapa, parasites alone kill hundreds of children every year. One day, as we walked by a local casket vendor, someone commented on the number of tiny

caskets on display. This may, in part, help you see how deep the need is there, but it is really greater than you can imagine. Again, it is impossible for me to give you the total picture.

So tonight I have conveyed four things about this trip, knowing all too well that you cannot fully grasp them: how you were so much with us in Guatemala, how much Christ was present as we ministered to the poor, how pure and genuine the worship was there, and how deep the need is now and will be in the future.

So where does this leave me, one who stands before you testifying of his mission experience, and where does this leave you who have heard my testimony? I can only speak for myself. Over the years, I have grown a bit skeptical of testimonies like this one, after retreats, mission trips, and the like. All too often the fire that is promised is not delivered. The effect lingers for a moment then is gone. There is no lasting impact. I have been guilty of this myself. So tonight I make no promises to you. Of course, my desire from this day forward is to be present with Christ, to do his work both in the temple and in the trenches. But my life from this day forward will be my true testimony. What has this trip meant to me? How has our trip affected you? We will write our answers with our deeds. Words are meaning-less unless actions follow.

O God, who is near to the brokenhearted, help us to remember how You brought us from darkness to marvelous light through Jesus Christ our Lord. Convict us by Your Spirit of our many sins, compel us by Your love toward humble service, and challenge us by Your Word to fulfill the purpose of our salvation: that the whole world may likewise know You and have fellowship with You, now and forevermore. Amen.

Chapter 19: Carnival Golf (Lesson 14)

October 22, 2014
5:10 pm

Jonathan,

As you know all too well, there are two golfers inside me, a bad one and a good one. The latter had been dormant for forty years until you recently awakened him from hibernation. I hit a few balls today, and I hate to inform you that I left this good golfer in Guatemala. In other words, I need a refresher course. Let me know when you are free to give a lesson. Until then, I will remain on my porch, waiting for the prodigal to come home.

Randy

Jonathan and I did meet early the next week, and I will share the details of that lesson below. Before I do, however, I want to warn you that this chapter could give you motion sickness. I invited you to join my golfing adventure at the end of chapter one. Since then, you have been my constant companion, a faithful back-seat passenger as Jonathan and I have moved closer to that July fork in the cart path. This is why I must give you fair warning. When the road gets bumpy, it's rare for the driver or front-seat passenger to get sick. The one vomiting into a bag is usually in the back, exactly where you are sitting. You are in a precarious spot if my game takes too many detours and turns.

Unfortunately for you, the route I am taking is as bumpy as a motocross event. Each week my game seems to vary wildly, at times ascending to new heights then descending to dark valleys. I'm up one day and down the next, on the smooth pavement after one lesson and off the shoulder into the ditch before the following one arrives. As a back-seat passenger, you have to endure every twist and turn, every climb and descent. While I am often nauseated about my game, I realize that you could be even more so watching me. I apologize sincerely. You have my permission to exit at the next stop.

It's not an exaggeration to compare my golf game to a carnival ride. Like a Ferris wheel or roller coaster, I am up then down, right then left, slow then fast, always returning to the place I started. In other words, it seems like I am going nowhere. The only way you can really understand what I mean is to ride along with me as I review my recent history. Any of you who are pregnant or have back and neck problems should step aside. I invite the rest of you to strap yourself into a seat next to me, swallow a Dramamine, and get prepared for the ride of your life.

Late September: "I am very low!"
Read Chapter 16 again if you need to be convinced. I was a golfer assailed by doubt, unsure if I would ever improve.

Early October: "I am very high!"
Scoring 87 at Cherokee Ridge put me on top of the world. Doubt vanished; hope abounded.

October 12-17: "I am higher than ever!"
My trip to Guatemala, as always, was a mountaintop experience. Golf was not even an afterthought.

October 22: "I am low again!"
My first attempts at swinging a golf club post-Guatemala were atrocious, leading to the SOS text message above.

October 27: "I am high once again!"
In just fifteen minutes on the range, Jonathan corrected my swing faults. I began to hit the ball crisply again, straighter than ever before. I was so on-target that he asked me to hit a small item 150 yards away. I almost did!

October 28: "I am low once again!"
I went to the range to reinforce yesterday's lesson, only to inexplicably descend to new levels of golfing futility. The same shots that soared straight and true were now dribbling off weakly to the right. How bad did it get? An older gentleman walked all the way from the opposite side of the range to give me a website address (rotaryswing.com) that might help my game.

October 28 (later that day): "Let's go even lower!"
I was hopeful that my performance on the range would not carry over to the course. Boy, was I disappointed! I played 27 holes, some of them horribly, recording scores of 51, 48, and 50 on the three nines. The same odd ball flight, short and dribbling off to the right, recurred over and over again. It was something I had not experienced yet with my new swing. I could not correct it, no matter how hard I tried. My ball striking from tee to green was

about as bad as I can remember, eerily reminiscent of the Shoal Creek Massacre. If not for an improved short game, the scores would have been much worse.

October 29 (today): "How low can you go?"
I went back to the range, hoping to find a cure for whatever is ailing me. As luck would have it, the range was closed for the day. I therefore returned to the golf course to do battle. The result was a score of 104 (52-52) that had the golfing demons howling in glee two days before Halloween. I had no pars and reached no greens in regulation. No other statistics are needed.

As I sit in the valley of today's performance, I am trying to make sense of it all. To be honest, I am having a hard time doing so. I realize that every athlete, amateur or professional, has good days and bad days. I know that a PGA tour player often records a low score and a high score on consecutive days. I understand that I am just four months into correcting five hundred months of faulty swinging. I am well aware that I am approaching sixty, the age when a golfer's performance tends to decline. I realize that golf is one of the hardest games to master and that Cherokee Ridge is tighter and more hazardous than the average layout. And I admit that my habit of strict scoring tends to put a negative spot-light on my game. Other golfers may quit keeping score when playing badly (a sure way never to score badly), but I continue to mark my card during the worst outings, yesterday and today being prime examples.

Such rationalization, however, can carry me only so far. An honest self-appraisal leads to the following conclusion: I am a bad golfer or a bad student or both. I am more inconsistent than my peers and not as amenable as they are to instruction. I have become a strange figure, a golfer I hardly recognize. My short game, once my weakness, is now my strength. My fairway woods, formerly my go-to clubs, are leading me astray. My "what does it really matter?" nonchalance has been replaced by a "what the heck is the matter?" lament. The only common thread between now and then is my scoring average, forever above bogey. I have become a golfing hypocrite, striking the ball one way on the range in Jonathan's presence but far differently when I am alone on the course.

I have so many questions now. Why is golf so different on the course than on the range? Is it my nerves? Is it the absence of Jonathan's voice, tweaking each little swing fault? Am I setting my sights too high? Is bogey golf from the blues at Cherokee Ridge beyond my potential, given my advancing age and limited natural ability? Am I Jonathan's eternal head-scratcher? Has his wonderful talent as a teacher met its match? Should I quit playing and scoring for now and limit myself to the range? If so, how do I know that I am practicing the right thing? Couldn't I make matters worse if I don't know what I'm doing wrong?

I have so many questions but no answers. And, for once in my life, I am at a loss for words.

****

Now that the roller coaster is back at its starting point, I am going to let you get off awhile to clear your head. Unfortunately, you have had to endure week after week the dizzying ups and downs that have defined my golfing journey. Saturday is the first day of November. From this point on, I will limit my updates to an end-of-the-month report. If you return to the carnival on December 1st, I will summarize my experience between now and then.

Who knows? Maybe I'll have an answer or two to share with you.

Chapter 20: A Lost Art (Lessons 15 and 16)

In my experience, golf balls are similar to teenagers. They are difficult to control. You have to approach them a certain way. They tend to navigate toward hazards. Once there, they hide when you try to find them. When found, they soon seek the hazards again. They seem to have minds of their own.

I am a golf ball's worst parent. Other golfers may keep their "children" in their bags a long time, but I lose mine quicker than the father lost the prodigal son. Unlike the Bible story, mine do not return. Thousands of golf balls have ignored my instructions and wandered off into woods, streams, lakes, and pastures. While searching for them, I have rescued hundreds of other golfers' lost balls and given them a new home in my bag. Despite the undeserved second chance, these ungrateful rebels drift away the next time they are placed on a tee.

My ability to lose golf balls sometimes defies explanation. During one round in my college days, a dog ran across the green and scampered away with my ball in his mouth. Golfers in other foursomes have sometimes discovered my wayward ball in their fairway and picked it up. By the time I have figured this out, they and my ball have moved out of sight. Just last year, I hit my drive in the right rough and then watched two skunks approach it and stop, as if laying claim to it. When they showed no signs of leaving, I walked down the opposite side of the fairway, placed a new ball on the green, and promptly three-putted. I gave myself a two-stroke penalty and recorded a stinking triple bogey.

Everyone who plays with me knows how rapidly I lose balls. As a result, golf balls have become the most frequent gift I have received over the past two decades. In December and January, when Christmas and my birthday come around and it's too cold to play, my golf bag becomes pregnant with dozens of balls. By Father's Day, however, I am in need of more dimpled gifts. Jeff, one of my best friends, has my name and a Bible verse imprinted on all the balls he gives me. These verses usually have a golfing and spiritual double meaning, such as "be still" and "straight is the way". Sadly, I have lost these balls, too, every single one of them. Golfers who find them must think I am both a lousy golfer and a religious fanatic. They are fifty percent right.

The reason it's so painful for a golfer to lose a golf ball is the fact that it's his or her own personal ball that is lost. In baseball, it's different. A batter who fouls a ball into the stands shrugs his shoulders because the lost ball is not his. It belongs to everyone playing the game. In contrast, a golf ball is a private possession. When it is marked with a Sharpie, its ownership is as clear and binding as a brand on a cow. Losing a golf ball, therefore, brings on angst similar to Barney Fyffe losing his badge. Golfers and bowlers are alike in this respect. They use their ball; nobody else does. Fortunately for bowlers, the ball is too big to lose and a gutter catches any rebel that tries to go astray. Golfers have no such luxury. Their ball is small enough to put inside their mouths, and the golf course has no collection area for errant shots.

The reason for this analysis of ball misplacement is the month of November, during which I lost more golf balls than ever before (which is saying a lot). My post-Guatemala slump continued, reaching new lows. Shots dribbled off to the right, never leaving the ground. Those that got airborne curved wickedly, also to the right, into whatever hazard happened to be there. I lost many, many balls. I don't have an exact number, but it had to be more than thirty. During one round, I reached into my bag for another ball and discovered that my pouch was empty. I spent the next fifteen minutes in the woods searching for a couple of balls, so that I could continue my round. Of course, I also lost these before the round was over. Thank goodness that Christmas, my birthday, and cold weather are just around the corner!

It is becoming obvious that Jonathan has a daunting task before him. I present him with challenges he most likely has never previously encountered. I am plagued by my past and perplexed by my present. As for the future, he continues to be upbeat and forward-looking. I, on the other hand, am in jeopardy of losing all hope, which is much worse than losing a thousand golf balls. My performance from tee to green is downright depressing, and my short game has not improved enough to compensate. As a result, my scores are going up, not down. The more I try to be a good student, the worse student I become.

The following correspondence between Jonathan and me will give you an indication of my fragile mental state this month and Jonathan's patient golf instruction and psychiatric counseling.

November 6 (after my fifteenth lesson)

Doc,

Great lesson today! Here's a recap for you.

1. A consistent approach to every shot before you take the club away is the only way to make consistent shots follow!

2. When you are trying to diagnose any issues with your ball striking for the full swing, consider for now that it is **either-or**. Examples are as follows. If **solidness of contact** is the issue, then the **upper body** is out of whack. If shots are hit solidly but errant in **direction,** then it is a **lower body** issue.

3. Below are six simple issues and fixes, assuming everything in the pre-shot routine is performed and you keep a fluid tempo.

Ball flight error	Swing Fix
Not solid, off to the right	Keep head stable and behind golf ball at impact
Not solid, off to the left	Keep head stable and move forward into impact
Not solid, thin	Keep chin stable instead of moving up and away
Not solid, fat	Keep chin stable instead of moving down
Solid and left	Get lower body going down target line, not left
Solid and right	Get lower body going down target line, not right

The above is a complete list of all the ball flights we saw today and the appropriate fix. Work on learning these shot patterns, recognize them as you see them, and reinforce the fix.

Happy hunting for that sub-80 round!

Jonathan

November 19

Jonathan,

At the end of our last lesson, everything seemed to be looking up. My post-Guatemala slump was over. I had a list of wonderful instructions from you about what to do if my ball was traveling this way or that. Golf was supposed to be fun again. The future seemed bright.

Since then, I have been to the range two times and to the course once (for 27 holes), and I hate to inform you that my game has gone southward again. As before, I have no explanation. On the range, I try to concentrate on doing things exactly as you say, but the results are so different. On the course, it's just as bad, sometimes worse. My recent nine-hole scores were 51-52-57.

The day I shot 87 at the Ridge seems long ago. I have regressed, and I don't know why. I want to fix it but don't know how. My immediate goal is to break 100 again. As the prophet said, "Woe is me!"

I know you have taught hundreds of golfers. Perhaps some of them have had a similar dip four months into their lessons. Maybe there is a way out of this dark valley. I hope there is.

For some reason(s), I cannot get my clubface square to the ball at impact. It seems to me that my problem lies totally in the downswing. If my set-up and takeaway are better than June, common sense tells me there has to be something terribly wrong with how I am getting my club from the top to the ball.

That is a question you can address at my next lesson. For now (and I am being serious for once), can you reassure me that I will be able to reach my goal by July? After my hour on the range today, I'm not so sure.

Randy

November 27 (after lesson sixteen)

Happy Thanksgiving, Master Teacher! I hope you have a great holiday with your family. I did practice and play at Cherokee Ridge yesterday. Overall, I hit the ball better. There were only 2-3 wild right shots. Most of my misses were left but well struck, something I can work with. I shot 100 (52-48) with 3 GIRs and 37 putts. I converted only 2 of 12 up-and-downs from less than 50 yards, so my short game had a lot to do with my score. It was the best I have hit the ball from tee to green since Guatemala. I am off suicide watch for now. – *Randy*

****

As I type these words, it is late afternoon on Black Friday. I have just completed eighteen holes at Cherokee Ridge. My score today of 108 (57-51) sadly reflects the state of my game as November draws to a close. I have played a total of 128 holes of golf this month and have averaged 104 per eighteen holes. My lost golf ball count now exceeds forty. What's more, I have lost any consistency and confidence I ever had.

It may seem from a golfing perspective that I have lost everything, but this is far from the truth. In fact, I will share this Thanksgiving weekend eighteen aspects of my golf game for which I am thankful:

1. I am thankful that I have not lost my golfing sense of humor.
2. I am thankful that I have not lost my willpower and resolve.
3. I am thankful that I have not lost all hope that I can reach my goal.
4. I am thankful that I have not lost my temper. (Okay, maybe once or twice, but can you blame me?)
5. I am thankful that I have not lost my clubs (but don't be surprised if my pitching wedge ends up in the bottom of a lake soon).
6. I am thankful that I have not lost Jonathan, my teacher. (May God give him patience and wisdom as he endures and assists this troubled student.)
7. I am thankful that I have not lost my mind (yet).
8. I am thankful that I have not lost my strict obedience to the *Rules of Golf*. (This will help me accurately gauge improvement in the future.)
9. I am thankful that I have not lost you, my reader. (You are still here with me, cheering me on. How frustrating all this must be to you!)
10. I am thankful that I have not lost my mathematical skills. (They have come in handy this month as I have calculated my scores.)

11. I am thankful that I have not lost my friends and family (for I am in desperate need of many small, round gifts.)
12. I am thankful that I have not lost my new grip, stance, and takeaway. (In spite of my present woes, I have not reverted to any of my old swings. I remain committed to the new swing, for better or worse.)
13. I am thankful that I have not lost the desire to play nine more holes every time a golfing day ends (yes, even today, after I shot 108).
14. I am thankful that I have not lost the thrill that comes when I hit a good shot or have a good hole.
15. I am thankful that I have not lost faith in the process. (I still have seven months left in this yearlong journey. Time is on my side.)
16. I am thankful that I have not lost perspective. (Golf is still a game, nothing more. Faith, family, friends, vocation, and health matter the most.)
17. I am thankful that I have not lost sight of the Shoal Creek Massacre. (Thoughts of that horrible day spur me onward in my quest for improvement. It was the lowest of all my golfing lows. Today doesn't compare.)
18. I am thankful that I have not lost a ball on the eighteenth green in my entire life. (In putt-putt golf, your reward for sinking the last putt is to lose your ball. This never seemed fair to me. In real golf, I end my round the same way, no matter how badly I have played: I remove my ball from the cup and place it inside my

bag. Every round, therefore, ends with a findable ball. I like that!)

I wonder what lies in store for me in December. Will November's miserable trend continue, or will improvement finally come? Will I be able to unlock the elusive secrets of the full swing? Will Jonathan spur me on to unprecedented heights, or will he lead me into further dark valleys before I see the light of day?

One thing is certain this yuletide season. My golf pouch will once again become pregnant with new balls. I am sure my friend Jeff will put a Bible verse on each ball he gives me. Maybe it will be this verse: "Well done, faithful servant!" And maybe, just maybe, the words will be true.

Chapter 21: Let the Tears Flow
(Lessons 17, 18, and 19)

I cry at the movies. Not all movies, mind you, but enough to label me sentimental. As I sit in the dark, something on the big screen triggers my lacrimal glands to fill my eyes with tears. It's not a wailing or a sob, just a moistening and a single drop streaking down one cheek. Still, it's in the crying spectrum. My family knows this all too well. Years ago, during poignant moments in movies, my youngest daughter, Allison, would often turn and look at my face. "Are you crying?" she would whisper. Absorbed in the moment and unable to speak, I would simply nod my head.

Not every emotional scene affects me this way. If it's a separation scene, having to do with people leaving each other, I am not moved one bit. During death scenes, divorce scenes, and soldiers-off-to-war scenes, I sit there with the cold-heartedness of a prison guard. I remember my wife sobbing aloud in the theatre during *Beaches*, when the mother died and her young daughter had to leave home. The only emotion I felt was embarrassment. I was afraid the viewers sitting near us would notice her.

Separation scenes, therefore, do not trigger an emotional release. Tear-jerkers for me are always reunion scenes. My all-time favorite weepy moment came during *Field of Dreams*, when Ray Consuelo, portrayed by Kevin Costner, reunited with his deceased father to play pitch and catch. Likewise, I remember crying during *Home Alone*, when the mother finally returned and embraced the son she left behind. The same thing happened during *It's a Wonderful Life*, when George Bailey, after deciding not to commit suicide, came home to family and friends. Believe it or not, I even had to wipe tears from my cheek when the three dogs returned in *Homeward Bound*.

When you think about it, every golf swing consists of a separation and a reunion. From the longest drive to the shortest putt, the clubface first moves away from the ball then returns to it. Consequently, given the pitiful state of my game at present, there are over a hundred separations and reunions during a typical round of golf. As with the movies, the separation (backswing) does not trouble me at all. Even a golf expert like Jonathan has no big issue with how I take the club back. It's not perfect, by any means, but it serves its purpose well: it gets the clubface ready for the return home.

Just like at the movies, it is the reunion (downswing) that has me in tears. No matter how hard I try, I cannot get the clubface back to the ball correctly. It's been a serious problem for two months and shows no sign of going away. I've spent hours searching the internet, listening to a dozen or more golf pros analyze the downswing, but I still don't know what I'm doing wrong. Jonathan's advice during lessons helps me correct the problem temporarily, but the effect doesn't linger. Apparently, he sees things I cannot see or feel. I improve in his presence but regress as soon as he is out of earshot.

Not surprisingly, my scores continue to suffer because of my downswing problems. I haven't broken 100 yet this month. My worst outing was a horrid 112, a performance so bad that it had me laughing at myself as I walked the course (probably a defense mechanism to keep me from crying). It is also not surprising that the vast majority of my time on the practice range and during lessons has been devoted to solving the downswing riddle. No surprise again, my short game has begun to regress due to neglect, which tends to inflate my scores all the more. It's a vicious cycle that I just can't seem to break.

To his credit, Jonathan has never lost his positive outlook and his enthusiastic demeanor. He is relentless, refusing to alter his original plan and to let my present doldrums change his style or approach. He reassures me that my situation is not unusual and that everything will soon begin to click. To his credit again, I have not lost faith in him or in the process and have refused to deviate from his instruction. I remain committed to the path he has set before me. If I do succeed, he should get all the praise for my transformation, just as God should get all the glory when a caterpillar becomes a butterfly. If I fail, the entire blame will fall on me, for the same reason that the canvas would have to be at fault if Rembrandt could not produce a painting.

With me as his student, Jonathan's genius has certainly been put to the test. At every lesson he tries to explain the downswing in a slightly different way, hoping that one day I will eventually see the light. By his own admission, he spends time between lessons thinking of a new approach to use with me. During lesson seventeen, he had me focus on moving my left hip toward the target just before beginning the downswing. The next week he had me separate the swing into two parts, concentrating on coiling my upper body during the takeaway and uncoiling my lower body during the downswing. Last week, during our nineteenth lesson together, we focused on using the larger core muscles instead of the smaller peripheral muscles throughout the whole swing. Each approach yielded positive results by the end of the lesson, but none of them helped the next time I hit range balls or played a round.

As we shook hands after lesson nineteen, Jonathan told me this would be the final golfing instruction of 2014. Although December was not half over, a hectic holiday schedule loomed ahead. Golf would have to take a back seat to family and festivities, as well it should. As he pulled off in his truck that day, I suddenly realized that this signaled the halfway point of my journey to July. Six months have passed since the Shoal Creek Massacre with six months to go.

An honest appraisal of my golf game at present gives cause for concern. I am almost as bad as I was during the June swoon and a long way from where I want to be. I have much ground to make up in order to reach my goal. Looking on the positive side, I am enjoying most aspects of this journey. I love analytics and am pleased that I'm beginning to understand what the golf swing should be. As a hospital physician, I am accustomed to diagnosis and treatment and am savoring the challenge of curing my golfing woes. I also cherish my friendship with Jonathan and look forward to each lesson with him. I even like practicing, something I never would have thought possible. But, on the negative side, I am still a miserable creature on the golf course. My scores are appalling, mostly because I cannot control the flight of my ball from tee to green. My short game is better but too inconsistent to make up for the deficiencies in my full swing. Unless the present trend changes, the choice of which fork to take in the path ahead will be an easy one.

****

Christmas of 2014 did come and go. On December 14, Cathy and I traveled to Mississippi to watch an amazing presentation of the Christmas story at First Baptist Church of Jackson. On the 23rd, the Stewart clan gathered in Tennessee for yuletide festivities at the home of my parents. Two days later, my wife's family did the same at her sister's house in Huntsville. Other holiday memories worth mentioning include the birthday of my mother, who turned 83 on Christmas day, and the wonderful news that both my daughters will give birth in 2015, raising the grandchild count to three.

The hectic Christmas schedule, combined with hospital duties and December's cold weather, would have made playing golf out of the question in past years. This year, however, was not the norm. Determined to keep my promise to work toward improvement, I braved windy and wet mid-forties weather to play four rounds of golf after lesson nineteen. True to form, my first score was 106 (56-50), my full swing continuing to be as unreliable as quicksand.

After the round, I retreated to the practice range to try to figure out (once again) what I was doing wrong. Shortly after I started hitting balls, I was joined there by Lane Gibbs, who had just finished his round. Knowing that Lane is an excellent golfer and a student of the golf swing, I began to share with him my frustration with golf in general and my game in particular. Instead of giving more advice, he recommended that I watch myself on video swinging a club. I consented, and over the next ten minutes he captured several swings on his iPhone. Then, in slow motion, he asked me to analyze what I saw.

As I watched my golf swing, two things stood out, one good and one bad. On the one hand, the first half of my swing was pretty solid: athletic setup, no head movement, good takeaway. I did notice my left elbow bending somewhat toward the end of the backswing, but only a little. My downswing, on the other hand, left a lot to be desired. The most obvious fault was my weight distribution: 60% on my right foot at impact. I was doing the opposite of all good golfers, who shift their weight predominantly to their left side by the time they strike the ball. It was a sure recipe for disaster.

With this knowledge fresh in my mind, I decided to quit thinking about my backswing and to focus instead on getting my weight to the left side at impact. I tried several swing thoughts, making sure they were consistent with Jonathan's teachings. Most of them created too much body and head movement and thus were not helpful. There was one swing thought, however, that seemed to work. If I concentrated on making a descending blow at impact (advice Jonathan had given in a previous lesson), crisp contact was restored and my distance and direction improved. It worked on the range that day. The question remained whether or not it would work on the course.

The next day I tested the new swing thought by playing a round at Cherokee Ridge. From the blue tees, in wet and cold weather, playing the ball down, putting everything out, and with strict adherence to the rules, I shot 90 (46-44). My ball striking from tee to green was vastly improved. I hit four greens in regulation and was near the green in regulation on seven more holes.

On the following day, I braved even colder and wetter conditions to play the same course from the same tees. I was anxious to see if concentrating on a descending blow would work on consecutive days. So many previous swing adjustments over the years had been one-round wonders, helpful today and hurtful tomorrow. I was fearful this would happen again. To my delight, my fears were unfounded. I shot 89 (43-46), including seven greens in regulation and seven near-GIR. My wife, who had witnessed several of my recent 100+ rounds, rode along with me. She was as amazed as I was at the improved ball striking from tee to green.

Not yet a true believer, I played again yesterday and shot 94 (49-45), hitting four greens in regulation plus five near-GIRs. Although not as consistent, my ball control from tee to green closely resembled the previous two rounds and was vastly better than recent weeks. I left the eighteenth green with a bounce in my step, and I am entering 2015 with renewed optimism.

I am convinced that at last I have solved the riddle of the downswing. After my club separates from the ball going back, it is now returning squarely at impact. A descending blow has made all the difference. But there may be yet another reason for my improvement: the return of the prodigal. After two long months away, the good golfer inside me has come home from Guatemala.

It's enough to make a grown man cry.

Chapter 22: Things to Do on a Wintry Day
(Lesson 20)

The first weeks of 2015 were colder than usual in Alabama, severely limiting my opportunity to practice or play. I had only one lesson with Jonathan the entire month. Faced with such poor weather conditions, I played no rounds of golf, restricting my time outdoors to the range and practice green.

Firmly committed to the task at hand, I was able to come up with the following indoor golf activities in January:

1. **I obtained a copy of the USGA's *Rules of Golf* and began to read it**. At the present time I am halfway through it, and I must admit that I have learned several things I did not previously know. My overall impression is that the *Rules* are fair but also a bit burdensome for amateurs like me. Without a doubt, most recreational golfers would have to add several strokes per round to their scoring average if these rules were followed to the letter. I am also convinced that the *Rules of Golf* did not originate in the nineteenth century, as golf historians attest. Instead, they must have been the work of a group of Pharisees in the first century. There is no other explanation for the multiple layers of regulations found in this little book. Only a Pharisee could have figured out so many ways to add a stroke or two to a hole or

even forfeit an entire round. Only a Pharisee could write rules in such a way that a physician would find them difficult to understand. Only a Pharisee, obsessed with the letter of the law, could make hitting a golf ball into eighteen holes the equivalent of Cinderella trying to please her stepmother.

2. **I started doing exercises targeted for golfers.** The internet is full of such activities, all designed to train golfing muscles and increase flexibility. I found a couple of routines that seemed fit for a 59-year-old and followed them during January. The soreness I felt in my muscles every day was further evidence that I had not been using them correctly over the past forty years. Whether or not these exercises will subtract strokes from my golf score is yet to be determined, but they have certainly succeeded in adding ibuprofen to my medical regimen.

3. **I practiced my putting stroke on the den carpet.** With the television blaring in the background and under the curious gaze of Sadie and Sam, my dogs, I rolled a ball over and over again on the rug, trying my best to keep it on a straight line. This helped to reinforce some things Jonathan has been emphasizing about putting: keeping my body still, my head down, and my takeaway and follow-through symmetric.

4. **I practiced chipping in my garage with a Nerf golf ball.** Using a throw-rug as practice turf, I launched balls toward the garage door, striving for the low

and straight trajectory that comes with a hands-first chip. It was a good way to concentrate on the proper chipping stroke without having to worry about the final result. I'm not quite sure how helpful it was, but it did serve to pass the time on a cold day. Since there was no emphasis on where the ball stopped in relation to a hole, my garage has been the only venue thus far where my pitching wedge and I are on speaking terms.

5. **I listened to instructors on the Golf Channel and Golf Academy.** I am aware that too many instructions from too many instructors can lead to too many swing thoughts. This, in turn, can lead to too many additional strokes on the golf course, the opposite of the intended goal. After six months with Jonathan, however, I knew his approach well enough to pay attention only to advice that was consistent with his teaching. All in all, listening to a variety of instructors helped me, because I was able to hear timeless golf concepts in different terminology. The more ways advice is presented to me, the greater the chance a golfing truth will penetrate my thick skull.

6. **I planned a golf vacation with one of my friends.** Michael and I share the same January birthday and have exchanged gifts every year for over two decades. Usually I purchase a book that would interest him, but this year I came up with something different: a Robert Trent Jones Trail Card for both of us. With this in hand, we can play the RTJ courses in Alabama in 2015 at a reduced rate. Our goal is to play a round at all eleven sites

this year, and Michael and I have already begun to coordinate our schedules to this end. This, of course, is a giant leap of faith on my part, for I am making the assumption that I will still be playing golf in July. Given the roller coaster ride that I experienced in 2014, this outcome is by no means certain.

7. **I spent a lot of time analyzing the progress of my game.** I recalled how frustrated I was after the Shoal Creek Massacre in June. I remembered the hope I felt when Jonathan answered my desperate plea for help. I brought to mind my first lesson with him and my feeble attempts to get my hands out in front of the ball at impact. I remembered how elated I was when I began to compress the golf ball for the first time and started to hit shots farther and crisper than ever before. I imagined once again the pride inside when I shot 87 at Cherokee Ridge. I winced when I recalled the self-doubt that flooded me after my trip to Guatemala, as my game inexplicably regressed. I thought of my recent return to pre-Guatemala form and the renewed hope inside of me. I thought about every bit of advice given me by Jonathan, about the patience he has shown in the midst of my struggles, and about the friendship we have forged during our months together as teacher and student. The end result of my month of introspection has been a sense of how far I've come and how thankful I am to have Jonathan by my side.

Going forward, the key to scoring below 90 is threefold: a more dependable full swing, an improved short game, and a commonsense course strategy. During our one lesson in January, Jonathan concentrated on the full swing, trying to help me discover why I was so inconsistent in ball striking. He told me that he had thought long and hard about my recent struggles with the full swing and had come to the conclusion that the inconsistency started when he tried to increase my lower body movement. With this in mind, he asked me to concentrate on two things that had worked well in August and September: a quiet lower body on the backswing and a stable shirt button on the downswing. The only swing thoughts he added were my hips moving toward the target just before the downswing and a descending blow on the ball at contact. By concentrating on these four things, I was able to trap the ball with my clubface, compress it, and send it forward on a reliable trajectory. Half of my outdoor golfing this month has been on the range, repeating these four swing thoughts stroke after stroke. The other half of my time has been spent at the practice green, trying to improve my putting and chipping. All in all, I think I have made some progress in January, in spite of the cold weather that has limited my golfing hours.

****

February now looms ahead. According to long-range forecasts, there is no guarantee that the weather will cooperate enough to permit a round of golf. If it does, there is also no certainty that the four swing thoughts above will be enough to turn the tide. I have no assurance that all my practice this month will transfer to the course. In this way (and this way only), my golf game and Tiger Woods' may be alike. Just yesterday, Tiger missed the cut in his first tournament of the year, shooting a dismal 82 on Friday. Part of his problem was an inconsistent full swing, but that was not all. His putting, once his strong suit, was so bad that golf analysts are now diagnosing him with the "yips". Tiger's preseason improvement on the range and putting green did not translate to the course during competition. During this week, at least, good practice did not yield good performance.

So it is with me. I am practicing well, but it remains to be seen what will happen when I step to the first tee. How will those four swing thoughts fare during the ups and downs of a round of golf? Will the extra work on my putting and chipping yield lower scores? An affirmative answer in my case is much less likely than for Tiger. He has a history of golfing greatness. I have a lackluster, sometimes laughable past. He is tweaking parts of his game, while I am overhauling all of mine. He may have had the "yips" last week, but I have had the "yikes" for forty years. My task in the next five months is to find a cure for this golfing malady. I must not let anything, even the cold of winter, stand in my way.

Chapter 23: Mind Games (Lessons 21 and 22)

Old Man Winter saved his strongest punch for February, when blasts of cold air from Siberia swept through Alaska and headed southeast into the interior states. Not even the South, including northern Alabama, was spared. The average high for this month is usually 58 degrees, but recent days have been twenty degrees below normal. Add wind, rain, ice, and snow to the mix, and you get a picture of the type of golfing weather I have endured.

That I played at all is a testimony to my desire to improve. I usually adhere to a "don't play unless it's over fifty degrees" rule, but desperate times call for extreme measures. If I am to reach my goal, I have to take advantage of every opportunity to practice and play. Braving the elements, I played five rounds of golf this month, including one with Jonathan, and spent more time on the range than usual. Not many golfers joined me. On most of these days, there were less than five cars in the parking lot when I arrived and none when I departed.

During my one range session with Jonathan, we concentrated again on the full swing. Using the four swing thoughts from January, I hit balls toward specific targets, trying to control both trajectory and distance. The results, in my opinion, were mixed, but I did hit several excellent shots and by the end of the session was able to fade or draw the ball whenever Jonathan asked.

Unfortunately, the optimism generated on the range that day was obliterated by my performance during the next two rounds. Using the same swing thoughts and supposedly the same swing, I had two plus-100 scores at Cherokee Ridge. The first was a very shaky 103 (53-50), the second a confidence-shattering 106 (54-52). Sub-fifty temperatures were not totally to blame. Substandard ball striking, once again, was the culprit.

I immediately texted Jonathan the bad news:

Jonathan,

The golfing news is not good. I walked 18 holes at CR yesterday and shot 103 (53-50). The score was no fluke. I played again today and shot 106 (54-52). It's hard for me to describe how inconsistent I was. I would hit a great shot, followed by two horrid ones. I tried to use the swing we worked on, but it produced good results only a third of the time.

Just for the heck of it, I also played a scramble today along with my regular ball. Hitting each shot twice and playing the best one, my score was 84 (41-43). The sizable 22-stroke difference between one-shot-me and scramble-me confirms that my main problem is a lack of consistency. In my opinion, there has to be something mental going on for there to be such a difference from range to course and from stroke play to scramble play.

I have to admit to you that I'm a little down right now. For the first time since last June, I find myself wishing that July would come so I could officially call it quits.

The vast difference in my game from the range to the golf course continues to plague me. It is one of the world's greatest mysteries, with no answer in sight, and it's getting old. I don't know what else to do but keep on trying... which I will do tomorrow.

I am telling myself to be upbeat, but I must confess that I have doubts about my ability to reach my goal. I need either a pep talk (to spur me on), a psychiatrist (to treat my depression), or a broken leg (to give me an excuse not to play).

I will continue to keep you updated on my "progress". The good news is this: it can't get much worse. Saturday will be too cold for golf. We'll schedule the next lesson when things warm up.

Your struggling pupil

Jonathan replied with characteristic optimism:

Doc,
We've got this!
1. Play to play great. Don't play not to play poorly.
2. Love the challenge of the day, whatever it may be.
3. Get out of results and get more into process.
4. Know that nothing will bother you or upset you on the golf course, and you will be in a great frame of mind for every shot.
5. Playing with the feeling that the outcome

doesn't matter is always preferable to caring too much.

6. Believe fully in yourself so you can play freely.
7. See where you want your ball to go before every shot.
8. Be decisive, committed, and clear.
9. Be your own best friend.
10. Love your wedge and your putter.

Jonathan

In all honesty, I was not encouraged by his Ten Commandments. "Easy for you to say," I thought. "If I shot in the low 70s like you do, I could be confident and positive when I stand over my golf ball." I began to wonder if it is possible for any good golfer to understand what it's like to be in my shoes. How can I expect the best on the course when I'm used to the worst? How is it possible to let nothing bother me when there's everything to be bothered about? How can I play as if the score doesn't matter when, in actuality, it matters a lot? It was the tenth commandment that upset me the most. "Are you serious, Jonathan?" I moaned aloud. "Is it really rational to love my wedge when it consistently treats me like an enemy?" What he was telling me to do seemed impossible.

As if sensing my frustration, Jonathan asked me to meet him at Chesley Oaks the following week to play a round together so that he could reinforce his Ten Commandments. On the front nine, as he watched me shoot a wayward 54 on an easy layout, he explained to me the mental approach I should have with every shot. In summary, this is his advice, what I now refer to as Jonathan's Theory of Positivity:

1. **Control.** "Golf is a game of controlled misses," Jonathan explained. "When you choose a club, you must choose the one that leaves you in the best shape if you hit it poorly. For example, if there's trouble past the green at 140 yards but not much trouble short, choose a club that's impossible for you to hit farther than 140 yards. This gives you a chance at a par or bogey at worst and eliminates the double or the dreaded triple."

2. **Commitment.** After I select the club and am ready to hit the ball, I must be 100% committed to the shot. There can be no wavering or doubting during a swing or putt, even if there seems to be good reason to waver or doubt. I must be totally committed to the decision I have made and must swing with ultimate trust in that decision, even if the decision turns out to be wrong. "It's okay to be wrong," Jonathan repeated over and over, "but it's not okay to be uncommitted."

3. **Confidence.** When I stand over a shot, I am to be so confident it will be good that I will be shocked if it isn't. It doesn't matter if it seems irrational or delusional to think this way; this has to be my mindset on every shot. "You know why the pros sometimes seem so cocky?" he asked. "Their confidence is so high that they naturally come across this way. Their swagger comes from their self-assurance."

4. **Compartmentalization.** I must separate each round into smaller compartments to maximize results. Furthermore, as I move from one compartment to the other, I must leave the previous one completely behind. In this way, I will protect myself from getting too low if I'm playing

poorly or too high if I'm playing well. Dividing the round into three-hole increments is one common way of compartmentalizing. Of course, the smallest compartment is the individual shot. If I treat each shot as a separate entity, not linked to anything that lies behind or ahead, then I am in the proper frame of mind to score well. "Frame of mind" is a great term, for each shot is like a single frame in a filmstrip. To have a good end result, Jonathan told me, I must "freeze-frame" each and every shot before me.

5. **Carefree.** As hard as it may be, I must stop caring so much about the score. I must be more process-oriented and less results-oriented. Why? Because I can control the process much more than I can control the results and because focusing on the process will ultimately lead to the desired results. "When I shoot my best rounds," Jonathan explained, "I often have no idea what my score is until the end. The results get placed on the back burner because I am wrapped up in the process. Focusing on the process will get rid of a lot of unnecessary anxiety, fear, and tension and will give you a better chance of scoring well."

After spending nine holes indoctrinating me in the Theory of Positivity, Jonathan asked me to put it into practice on the back nine. I was convinced that I had nothing to lose, so I went ahead and played the mind game Jonathan had described to me. Before each shot, I picked the club that would put me in the least trouble if I mishit it. Once I made that choice, I became 100% committed to that club and to the shot at hand, refusing to let doubt enter my mind. After I hit the ball, I confidently expected it to be right on target. Throughout the back nine, I compartmentalized my game, taking each shot as a single frame of reference, refusing to be swayed by past successes or failures. Lastly, I played those nine holes without much regard to the score, concentrating instead on the process Jonathan had laid out for me. The result was a decent 45, nine strokes better than the front nine. By believing in Jonathan's Theory of Positivity and obeying his optimistic Ten Commandments, both my ball striking and scoring improved without any attempt on my part to change my technique.

Truly, the mind is a very powerful force and, as the commercial says, is a terrible thing to waste. I remember a lecture in medical school on hypnosis, during which the instructor hypnotized several members of my class. He told one student to yell "Roll Tide!" when a particular word was later said. He informed another student that she would feel a cigarette burn when she was awakened from hypnosis. I then watched two of the brightest people in Alabama do just as he said. Immediately after snapping out of the hypnotic state, the female student began to rub her forearm and wince in pain. When asked why, she claimed to have suffered a cigarette burn. Even more incredible, a small circular wound could be seen on her forearm. A few minutes later, when the professor said the previously mentioned word, I heard the male student shout "Roll Tide!" like a cheerleader, without a clue as to why he did so.

If the mind, in both its subconscious and conscious components, is so powerful and persuasive, then Jonathan may be right. Perhaps the positive power of suggestion is a necessary tool for playing my best golf and reaching my goal. Delusional or not, I have to give it a try.

Until further notice, then, I will consider a proper frame of mind to be an essential part of my game. It will be the fifteenth club in my bag, one I will use with every shot.

Remember my "swing thoughts of a bad golfer" from chapter three? In keeping with Jonathan's Theory of Positivity, I have rewritten them as follows:

> **Any golf ball will do** has been amended to **only one golf ball will do**. (In the future, I will play one ball and one ball only: a yellow Pinnacle—because yellow is my favorite color, because I live on Pinnacle Point, and because I'm sure I will hit that low-rent ball very well.)

> **I must feel my way around the course** has become **I will control the way I feel around the course**.

> I no longer **play fast**; instead, I **play positive: controlled, committed, confident, and carefree**.

> Previously, **I hit my woods better than my irons**. Now, **I hit my woods and irons better than ever**.

> No longer will I complain that **I play worse as I get closer to the hole**. My new mantra is this: **I can't wait to get close to the hole!**

> **I need to change my swing now** has been replaced by **I need to trust my swing now**.

> **People tend to play well when I'm around** has been transformed to something more positive: **my playing partners will see some great shots from me today!**

> **I appreciate that piece of advice** will soon become **let me give you a piece of advice**.

A sand trap is my worst nightmare is now false. The new truth is this: **a sand trap is a dream with a happy ending**.

I used to complain, **"Bogey putts fall. Par putts fail."** From now on, I will proclaim, **"All putts have a chance to drop, and many will."**

Perhaps the law of averages will come into effect on my next shot has been restated thusly: **Surely, the Theory of Positivity will work its magic on my next shot**.

The former false hope that **whatever worked today will work tomorrow** is now the gospel truth: **whatever worked today *will* work tomorrow... and every day thereafter**.

Jonathan ended the teaching session with a compliment and a challenge. "You have a full swing and short game that should enable you to shoot in the low-to-mid 80s," he told me. "The reason you aren't is mental, not technical."

"Are you sure?" I replied. "I don't want you to say something just to make me feel good. I want the truth."

"I am not stretching the truth at all," he assured me. "Of course, there are things I will continue to tweak in your game, but not anything drastic. Today, right now, you have the swing of a sub-90 golfer. I don't think you will shoot below 80 from the blue tees at Cherokee Ridge. You've made it a bit hard on yourself by setting your scoring goals from those tees. In my opinion, you would be better off teeing it forward, because you would immediately score better and enjoy it more. Regardless,

175

your technique is sound enough to shoot 85 from the blues at the Ridge, but it won't happen until you conquer your mental demons."

I left the course that day with a promise to him and to myself to do just that. During the following week I played three rounds of golf, two in Mississippi and another at Cherokee Ridge, in some of the most brutal winter weather conditions I have encountered in my golfing career. The bad news, in addition to the elements, was my short game. In all, I converted only 15% of my up-and-down chances from less than fifty yards. The okay news was my scoring: rounds of 91, 89, and 94. Under normal weather conditions, I am certain these would have been three to five shots less. Even better news was my ball striking. Without a doubt, my performance from tee to green on all three days was more consistent than at any time in recent weeks. But the greatest news by far was my mental game. As promised, I played each round in keeping with Jonathan's Theory of Positivity, obeying his Ten Commandments on each shot. The results, needless to say, were positive, and now I am totally onboard the Positive Mind Train. What once was theory has now become law.

Want to know how positive I am? Yesterday evening, while my wife was staying with her grandmother and I was home alone with the dogs, I went to the garage, located my golf bag, and gently pulled one of my irons from its resting place. Looking straight into the grooves on its face and fighting back tears, I softly whispered to my pitching wedge, "I love you!"

I am, indeed, a changed man.

Chapter 24: Forkless (Lesson 23)

March has come and gone, and I am now nine months into my yearlong quest to improve in golf. But as flowers bloom, temperatures rise, and optimism abounds, I find myself relatively indifferent about golf in general and my game in particular. I am suffering from what I call the 75% Syndrome, a mixture of burnout, apathy, and second-guessing that arises three-fourths into any lengthy endeavor. It's what I experienced at mile eighteen of the two marathons I have completed. I felt the same way at the end of my third year of medical school. Expectant mothers probably go through similar emotions thirty weeks into their pregnancies. I bet Christopher Columbus was beset by the same melancholy three-fourths into his voyage. I imagine him complaining, "I've come too far to turn back, but I'm still so far from dry land!"

Like Columbus, I have had to navigate turbulent seas this past month. Some of these storms have been external. Indeed, I have endured more than my quota of rain, wind, and cold. But the majority of the tempests that I have dealt with have been internal: indifference, malaise, and mental fatigue. Although I am certain that April will signal the end of winter's grip, I have no such guarantee that my weather-torn psyche will likewise be reborn. Unless I become proactive and confront this melancholy, my golf game will wither while nature blossoms around me.

The cure for the 75% Syndrome is three-fold: awareness, endurance, and hope. I must be aware of what is going on inside me, must be willing to endure it as long as it lasts, and must be hopeful that it will soon pass away. Having dealt with this before in marathons and medical school, I know full well what I must do in the weeks ahead. I must push myself forward and continue to play golf like it matters a lot, even when it doesn't seem to matter much at all.

This I have done. Remaining faithful to the process, I played six rounds of golf in March, in spite of my lack of incentive to do so. On every shot I applied the psychology Jonathan recommended. I was positive, committed, and process-oriented, not as concerned with the score from hole to hole and thus not as emotionally labile. Even though my scores didn't improved all that much (average: 93.6), I am convinced more than ever that my game is beginning to turn around.

My stats for the six rounds reveal what I need to do to reach my goal of sub-90s golf. My driving (three added strokes per round) and putting (four added strokes) are still my strengths. They are good enough right now to carry me to my goal. My approach shots and short game, however, are holding me back. On the average, poor approaches add six to seven strokes to my eighteen-hole score. Even worse, bad pitching and chipping add an average of eight strokes to my scorecard. If Jonathan can help me improve my approach, my pitch, and my chip, good days lie ahead. In light of this, I predict that my year of lessons will end where it began: at the practice green with Jonathan teaching me the short game.

****

Although we intended otherwise, Jonathan and I were able to meet for just one lesson this month. One of the reasons was the inclement weather. March was colder, wetter, and windier than average, especially on days we had a lesson planned. But there were other factors that kept us apart, matters of life and death. On the very same day, both of us experienced life-altering family events, and golf became to us a secondary concern.

On the fourth of March, I was sitting in a family waiting area at Baptist Hospital in Jackson, Mississippi. My youngest daughter, Allison, was in labor with our second grandchild. Our hopes were high, our spirits soaring.

This time of joyful waiting was interrupted by a text message from one of my golfing buddies, informing me that Jonathan's brother-in-law, only in his early forties, had been killed in a motor vehicle accident in Georgia. I felt immediate sadness for Jonathan's wife, Kelly, and for her parents, realizing they had just lost their only brother and son. I called Jonathan to express my love and support. After the call, I offered a silent prayer that God would comfort and strengthen them.

As I returned my focus to my granddaughter's imminent birth, my mind was flooded with memories of a similar recent tragedy. Kelly's sudden loss of her brother rekindled raw emotions from 2013, when my younger sister, Karen, died of complications of pneumonia. We were only one year and one day apart in age and had

179

shared everything growing up: birthday parties, sicknesses, schools, etc. When she suddenly lapsed into a coma and died four days later, my parents, siblings, and I likewise grieved her loss and longed for God's embrace.

During the next two hours in the waiting room, my thoughts alternated between birth and death. I thought of Kelly and her brother. I thought of Karen and me. I thought of Allison's new baby girl. I also thought of the daughter she lost at twenty-two weeks in a previous pregnancy. I was reminded of the beauty and brevity of life, how fragile and fleeting it can be. Although I see this every day in my hospital work, what I experienced on March 4 was more personal and its effect on me more profound.

As would be expected, the birth of beautiful Caroline Catherine and the death of Jonathan's brother-in-law made golf seem insignificant, which magnified even more the effects of the 75% Syndrome. I began to have second thoughts about devoting so much time, emotion, and energy to a ball-and-stick endeavor instead of focusing more on matters of flesh-and-blood. I started to view my yearlong golfing journey as superficial and peripheral to what's really important in life. Looking at golf from life's perspective, I began to value the friendships I have made on the course more than the numbers I have written on my scorecard.

As I sat there, waiting to be a granddad again, many wonderful golfing memories flooded my mind, none of them tied to a score.

I remembered the laughter...

...of Terry Williams and Everett McAnally, my best high school friends, after I swung and missed on the first tee at Bigby Hollow. (Everett and I were preacher's kids, and Terry was a faithful Christian. On the football team, we were referred to as the God Squad.)

...of Jeff Fowler and me, when we got lost on our way to play at Quail Creek and ended up at the wrong course. (That trip twenty years ago forged a friendship more valuable than gold, one that has taken us to Alabama-Mississippi State football games, to numerous Alabama golf courses, even to the mountains of Guatemala. As you recall, the FedUp Cup was our idea.)

...of Greg Driskill and Robert Page, two ER physicians, when I scored a 13 on an over-the-water par three at Limestone Springs. (I was like Kevin Costner in *Tin Cup*, hitting ball after ball into the hazard, ignoring their repeated invitations to stop, until one at last landed on dry land.)

I remembered the conversations...

...with Michael McGee at Twin Lakes, as we tried to solve the world's problems. (From hole to hole, we moved from topic to topic: faith, family, football, food, and fitness, to name a few. Our friendship didn't begin on the golf course, like mine and Jeff's, but it was built there. By the way, if you happen to see Michael, ask him about the magnificent 3-wood approach shot he hit on the eighteenth hole at the Kapalua course in Maui during a family vacation together.)

...with my dad and my brother as we played Kenny Perry's Country Creek. (I can still recall most of what we said on those days, but I can't recall what we shot. Telling, isn't it?)

...with Mary Catherine and Allison, my two daughters, as they accompanied me on a few rounds of golf. (Their demeanor on the course mirrored so much their personalities in life. Mary Catherine, older and more analytical, concentrated on hitting the ball correctly. For Allison, younger and carefree, the primary goal was to break the tee in half as she swung, a feat she finally accomplished at age twelve, after which she retired from golf.)

And I remembered the tears...

...of joy, as we celebrated during a round of golf the various milestones in our lives—birthdays, promotions, anniversaries, etc.

...of laughter, at each other and at ourselves, when our golfing futility descended to the level of comedy.

...of sorrow, as we gathered in a circle on the first tee of Chesley Oaks to pray for Brian Taylor, our friend and golfing buddy, who was battling terminal pancreatic cancer.

I then thought of other golfers who have impacted my life in such a positive way—Barry Guess, Ron Lynch, Harlice Keown, Allen Walworth, Mike Moore, Craig Young, and Bo Morgan. I began to appreciate once again what golf has brought to me through them. Sadly, I had forgotten that the most important thing on the golf course is not the putter in my hand but the friend at my side. Determined to improve my game, I had changed my entire focus to the numbers rather than the names on my scorecard. I had placed the challenge of playing bogey golf ahead of the privilege of playing golf with my buddies.

I have thus made a pivotal decision about my golfing journey, one that brings everything into proper perspective. My wife, it turns out, has been right all along. She has predicted for many weeks that I will continue to play golf even if I fail to reach my goal. Stubborn and proud, I have rebutted her each and every time. But now, after being reminded what matters most in life, I have come to the conclusion that the greatest golfing mistake I could make in July would be to abandon the golfing friendships I have enjoyed over the years. The conversations, comradery, and comedy we share during each eighteen holes are glorious privileges that should be highly cherished. The pain of a 98 on my scorecard pales in comparison.

Don't be mistaken. I still remain committed to my task. Going forward, I will continue my quest for improvement, trying my best to be the best golfer I can be. I will keep my scoring goals the same. But I will withdraw this silly threat to give up golf forever if certain scores aren't achieved. According to historians, Columbus came ashore hundreds of miles south of his intended goal. Still, his journey was considered a success. Should my golfing journey be any different?

The road I am traveling is the same as last month, but something now is different. No longer is there a fork ahead in the cart path, no diverging branch leading to a golfing dead end. The sign that says *Left Lane, No Golf* has been removed, for that pathway has been barricaded. I have eliminated that option once and for all. *Golf* is the now the only avenue before me, one I will gratefully travel even if it becomes littered with scores I never intended. I have too much to lose if I don't continue to play.

Chapter 25: An April Diary (Lessons 24 and 25)

Wednesday, April 1

Jonathan and I had a lesson scheduled today at Stoney Mountain Golf Course, which is by far the worst eighteen-hole layout in the county. Even when freshly mowed, it resembles a pasture on which several flags have been erected. Because of the recent rainy weather, today's course conditions were especially poor.

I chose this venue for our lesson for two reasons: it was on my way home from clinic, and its sparse traffic would allow plenty of time for teaching as we walked nine holes.

Unfortunately, Jonathan could not make the lesson, so I had to navigate the pasture alone. We had planned to concentrate on my short game, and my performance showed how desperately I need this. My pitching and chipping were very shaky, and my putting was a bit off as well. I didn't keep score, which probably turned out for the best. Sadly, the quality of my game today matched the quality of the course.

Thursday, April 2

I played eighteen holes at Cherokee Ridge, my wife riding along with me. I shot 95 from the blues, still above-bogey golf. My approach shots, pitching, and chipping were my downfalls, a continuation of yesterday's trend. Driving and putting were okay but not good enough to compensate for my approach-pitch-chip woes.

This has been a recurring theme of late. I am usually in position to go for the green in regulation, but my approach is not accurate enough to land the ball on the green. As a result, I usually find myself close to the green but not on the putting surface. From there, my short game is not good enough to save strokes. In fact, I often add more strokes with poor pitches and chips. It is becoming obvious that my short game needs to become my focus from this moment forward.

Friday, April 3

Today I played my first round of the year with some of my golfing buddies. Barry, Ron, Charlie, and I traveled to Guntersville State Park and completed eighteen holes in winds resembling those experienced at the British Open. The scores, higher than usual for all of us, were as follows: Barry 89, Ron 89, Charlie 90, Randy 97. I was the most consistent, most accurate, and often the longest driver of the group. My approach shots were comparable as well. From tee to green, therefore, I was on the same level with my partners. My short game, once again, was my nemesis. This included a horrible putting performance to go along with my usual pitching and chipping troubles. Every stroke separating my partners and me was attributable to their short games being better than mine.

Here's my take on today's round. From a scoring standpoint, nothing seems to have changed from years past. I remain 5-10 strokes worse than my peers and have a poor short game to blame. In addition, my mental toughness is still not equal to theirs. But, believe it or not, I am not dismayed. Several things *are* different this year that give me reason for hope. I now have one swing, not four versions of a swing. My tee-to-green performance with this one swing is improving every month. My putting, other than today, is better. My short game deficiencies should be correctable with proper teaching and consistent practice. And my lack of mental toughness can be easily cured if I make mental focus mandatory, not optional.

One mental breakthrough did happen today. At the end of my round, I came to the conclusion that improvement from this day forward is completely in my court. Granted, I still need Jonathan's guidance and instruction, for I have much more to learn and major hurdles to leap. But now that the foundation for improvement has been laid by him, I am the only one who can build on it. Starting today, therefore, I am placing the onus of improving my golf game squarely on my shoulders. To bring my scores into the 80s, I must be assertive and take the necessary steps. My first move will be to spend more time focusing on my short game.

Monday, April 5

I practiced my short game at Cherokee Ridge. The weather was a bit cool, so I wore a sweater vest zipped to my upper chest. As I chipped and putted, I concentrated on whether the dangling zipper handle on my chest moved during the stroke. I soon discovered that I had veered off course by not following one of Jonathan's essentials. I had not been keeping the second button on my shirt motionless during a pitch, chip, or putt. When I corrected this oversight, I immediately became more consistent in my short game.

Tuesday, April 7

More short game practice today. I'm beginning to feel a bit more comfortable with pitching, chipping, and putting. The secret right now is a stable, motionless chest throughout the shot. If the second button of my shirt doesn't move right, left, forward, or back, I usually make solid contact. If it moves only one inch in any direction, the result is adversely affected by several feet.

Friday, April 10

I walked the front nine at Cherokee Ridge today and played the best golf of the calendar year. All aspects of my game were clicking, even my much-maligned short game. The score of 42, respectable enough, does not reveal how well I played. My putting let me down on two holes, but my pitching and chipping were so much better. Apparently, my short game practice is paying dividends. May the trend continue!

Tuesday, April 14

Barry, Charlie, and I played at Chesley Oaks today. The ground was soaking wet, and the wind was howling (the norm in 2015). For this reason, the course played tougher than usual. I shot 91, Charlie 89, and Barry 83. The difference was Barry's superior short game. This, unfortunately, continues to be the same sad tale. I have the tee-to-green game of a mid-80s golfer but the short game of a high-90s golfer. This is why I am still scoring higher than bogey golf. Admittedly, I have noticed some improvement in my short game during practice sessions, but this has not yet translated to the course when playing with my group. The bottom line is this: when Barry and Charlie are eyewitnesses to my improved short game, I will achieve my scoring goal, and not one moment sooner.

<u>Wednesday, April 15</u>

I played at Cherokee Ridge today. Once again, my ball striking was good enough. I was on the green in regulation on five holes and near the green in regulation on nine others. But my short game again was my nemesis. I converted only two of twelve up-and-down opportunities. The result was a predictable score of 92.

Looking on the positive side, my flat stick was good today. I had only 32 putts, thanks to improved green reading and distance control. In addition, my driving and approach shots were decent. They were good enough to propel me to my scoring goal.

But then there's the negative. Have I mentioned yet that my pitching and chipping have to improve if I am going to break 90?

Chapter 26: Falling in Love Again (Lesson 26)

92, 94, 92.

This is the answer to the question, "How is your golf game this time post-Guatemala?" Since I returned from there on May 9, these are my three scores at Cherokee Ridge, all respectable and in the low 90s but still above bogey golf. The positive news is that the good golfer inside me decided to make the return flight this trip. The not-so-good news is that the bad golfer did, too. In essence, nothing has changed. I am the same now as I was at the end of April.

From a scoring standpoint, then, nothing is different. But that is not the whole story. As I look back to June of 2014 and compare what I was then to what I am now, quite a bit has changed. The way I play and perceive the game is different. No longer do I migrate from one swing to another during the course of a round. No longer do I avoid the practice range and green. Gone are the days of utter frustration and futility on the course. Instead, my love for the game has reached new heights, so much so that bad scoring days are considered good just because golf is involved.

How do I love golf? Let me count the ways. I love the natural beauty seen on the course, the wonderful fellowship enjoyed during a round, the life lessons mirrored in the game itself. I love the immense challenge of the full swing, the subtle variables of the short game, and the inner "yes!" of a great shot or putt. I love the peace and calm of a round played in solitude and the sound of clubface on ball that breaks that silence. I am one of those golfers who always leaves the eighteenth green wishing there was one more hole to play. I consider myself blessed. Many people spend entire lives seeking an enjoyable pastime. I found mine forty-five years ago on a golf course with my dad. I am truly thankful that I have such a passion for the game.

Speaking of Dad, I traveled to Tennessee this month to see him. The reason for the trip was a belated Mother's Day celebration, so Dad was not my primary focus. Nevertheless, he accompanied us to lunch and, as usual, garnered his share of the attention. After a recent fall at another restaurant, he now reluctantly uses a walker due to severe degenerative arthritis of the back, hips, and knees. His mind, however, seems younger than his 89 years, and his faith in God and love for his son are eternal.

In addition to his joint problems, Dad's hearing has also deteriorated. Since he is too proud (i.e. stubborn) to wear hearing aids, his auditory enhancer has become the remote control in his hand. He will sit for hours watching sports events at decibels that would register on a seismograph. Communication with him has become increasingly difficult. We have been told since childhood not to yell at our parents. Now, as an adult, I have no other choice.

This time of year is the best of all for watching and listening to TV sports. Surfing the channels, you can see baseball, basketball, spring football, hockey, and soccer, all in a single day. But golf is my Dad's favorite, and I have spent several days with him in the past year listening to golf announcers who seem to be yelling as they whisper.

In my parents' living room, golf is not a quiet game. It's louder than being at the Super Bowl or World Series.

This brings me to another reason I love golf: its uniqueness. No two sports are alike, but golf is more unlike the rest. How? Again, let me count the ways. In fact, I will list eighteen ways golf is unique, one for each hole on the course (also one for every stroke I am over par at the end of a round).

1. <u>The lowest score wins.</u> Only in golf is being less considered greater. Only on a golf course is a subpar performance praised, a negative on the scoreboard deemed positive.

2. <u>Anyone can compete with anyone.</u> Thanks to different tees and the handicap system, I could play a competitive round with Rory McIroy, the greatest golfer in the world, and he would not have to alter his game one bit. This would be impossible in other sports. Can you imagine yourself and Roger Federer on a tennis court? Unless he played blindfolded and left-handed, you wouldn't have a prayer.

3. <u>A golfer is his own referee.</u> Does a pitcher ever call a balk on himself? Have you ever seen a basketball player hand the ball to his opponent after double-dribbling? Does an offensive lineman admit to holding when no one else notices? This type of self-policing goes on all the time in a round of golf. How many times can you remember yelling at a referee during a golf tournament? Zero. Because referees don't exist. That's unique, isn't it?

4. <u>Silence is expected.</u> The crowd at a basketball game can yell and wave towels during a free throw, but just one

peep or move by a spectator during a putt is frowned upon.

5. <u>The playing field differs.</u> Every golf course is unique. In contrast, the dimensions of basketball and tennis courts and of soccer and football fields are identical. Baseball fields, like golf courses, are not all alike, but the difference is limited to the depth of the outfield and the width of foul territory. In golf, from tee to green and everywhere in between, no two holes anywhere are exactly the same.

6. <u>You can play when you're very old.</u> I haven't heard of an octogenarian hockey league, an "old geezers" soccer tournament, or a tackle football game between great-grandfathers. In contrast, senior golfing leagues can be found all over the world.

7. <u>The ball is struck with several sticks.</u> A golfer can carry fourteen clubs onto the course and is allowed to use all of them during a round. A baseball, tennis, or hockey player is limited to one bat, racket, or stick while competing.

8. <u>The ball is motionless when struck.</u> In fact, a golfer is penalized if his or her ball moves after address. In other major sports, the ball or puck is usually in motion when struck.

9. <u>There is no stereotypical golfing frame.</u> Basketball players are tall and lean. Football players are muscular and thick-necked. Hockey players have missing teeth. There are no fat professional tennis or soccer players, no slim offensive linemen. But PGA golfers come in all shapes and sizes: muscular (Tiger Woods), rotund (Craig Stadler), short (Jeff Sluman), and tall (Bubba Watson). It is

a true statement that everyone you meet at work or greet at church is built like a professional golfer.

10. <u>Snakes and alligators can be encountered.</u> I have also seen skunks, geese, deer, lizards, and pelicans. A dog on a baseball field is captured and removed. A deer at a basketball or hockey game would be totally unexpected. Wildlife and golfers, however, share the same habitat. They coexist on the course and are content to leave the other alone.

11. <u>You can write on the ball.</u> Marking a golf ball with a Sharpie is recommended. If you doodled on a baseball, the umpire would toss it aside.

12. <u>The announcers are on the course.</u> In all other sports, play-by-play is given from outside the playing field, usually in a press box. Golf reporters, however, are often inside the ropes, right where the action is.

13. <u>Golf is a four-letter word.</u> No other major sport can make this claim. Fittingly, no other sport tends to turn the player into a four-letter mutterer.

14. <u>Motorized vehicles are allowed.</u> With rare exceptions, golf carts are mainstays on courses. No other major sport permits motorized vehicles on the field of play during competition.

15. <u>No night games.</u> Golf is the only major sport played only in daylight.

16. <u>Opponents do the same thing.</u> In every major sport except golf, competitors are doing different tasks. When one is on offense, the other is on defense. One punts; the other receives. As one team moves from fielding to batting, the opposing team moves in the opposite direction. It's different in golf. Opponents do the very

same activity as they compete. They hit their drives, approaches, chips, and putts alongside each other. It's not as synchronized as Olympic swimming, but it's certainly a step in that direction.

17. <u>A caddy is allowed to carry equipment and offer advice.</u> In tennis, coaching is not permitted during a match. In football, a coach is not allowed on the field during a play. In hockey, a player cannot have a constant companion skating alongside him carrying his stick, gloves, and false teeth. In golf, such a companion is the norm.

18. <u>Communities are built because of golf.</u> Have you ever heard of a soccer community or a hockey community? What about a baseball or football community? In contrast, golfing communities are common, like the one in which I have resided for the last seven years.

If you need more evidence that my attitude toward golf has made a 180-degree turn, then consider my recent trip to The Tradition. This event, one of the PGA Senior Tour majors, was held this month at Shoal Creek Golf Course near Birmingham, the site of the infamous Massacre at Shoal Creek that I endured last June. As I watched the senior pros play the course that brought me to the brink of quitting, I actually felt no ill will, suffered no flashbacks, and had no inner rush of inferiority. I no longer viewed it as a torture chamber but as a wonderful golfing venue. The guy at the security gate, whom I had deemed both warden and executioner last June, was now considered a friend, not a foe. Had I seen my caddy, that guy from Wisconsin who was an accomplice to the Massacre, I am convinced that I would have hugged his neck.

My true helper, Jonathan, was able to carve time out of this month's busy schedule for a lesson. His sole focus on that day was my short game. I spent two hours hitting shots from one hundred yards and shorter. I learned which club to use at 100 yards (a choked-up 9-iron), 85 yards (a full pitching wedge), 70 yards (a choked wedge), etc. I learned (but failed to master) the difference in using the leading edge versus the bounce of a wedge on short shots. I discovered that several bad habits had crept back into my swing. I heard Jonathan stress once again the importance of mind and attitude in golf, urging me to quit being a mental midget on the course, especially when I'm playing with a group.

Time is now running out. Only one month remains in my yearlong quest for improvement. Much about my golf game is different, yet my score remains the same. I'm like the fat guy who diets but doesn't lose weight. I'm doing all the right things but not seeing the results where it matters. But I have not in any way given up hope. I feel I am on the verge of a breakthrough. I still believe that my scoring will improve soon and that my goals will be met.

The reason I feel so confident is one piece of advice Jonathan gave me at the end of our lesson, something he said that I had never previously heard, something simple yet profound, something practical and easy to apply. I sincerely believe that this golden nugget will propel me beyond the above-90 hump into the joy of 80s golf.

What is this piece of advice? I'm not going to reveal it to you now. Sometimes there is added power in keeping a truth to oneself, and I need all the power I can muster. I doubt even Jonathan knows what he said this month that has my hopes so high. I'll let him and you in on the secret as soon as June, and with it my twelve-month challenge, comes to an end.

Chapter 27: A Better Obsession

As far back as I can remember, I have been fascinated with numbers. During my childhood, I tried to count to one million on school notebook paper. I made it to one hundred thousand before boredom ruled the day. As an adult, I have made it a habit to memorize telephone numbers, even those stored away in my iPhone. I also enjoy keeping up with a lot of other numbers: miles to my destination, days until an event, calories consumed, etc. Although I don't have a clinical diagnosis of Obsessive-Compulsive Disorder, when it comes to numbers I am definitely residing in the suburbs of OCD-ville.

For better or for worse, golf is a game of numbers. Every course is a combination of three, four, and five pars. Every golfer can rattle off his or her driving distance, handicap, or favorite yardage. Every ball has a number stamped on it, every hole has a number assigned to it, and every club has a number engraved into it.

The most important number in golf, of course, is the score at the end of eighteen holes. Not surprisingly, I have made my personal score an obsession, striving to consistently break 90 at my home course. To this day, this obsession remains unfulfilled. Even after a year of lessons, I remain a bogey golfer.

Listed below are my eighteen-hole golf scores the past twelve months at Cherokee Ridge, in groups of four:

| 91 | 95 | 93 | 95 | (average: 93.5) |
| 89 | 87 | 99 | 104 | (average: 95.0) |

103	100	112	106	(average: 102.75)
92	90	89	94	(average: 91.25)
103	106	94	93	(average: 99.0)
89	91	91	96	(average: 91.75)
95	91	92	92	(average: 92.5)
92	94	92	93	(average: 92.0)
92	94	95	89	(average: 92.5)
94	89	92	95	(average: 92.5)

Here are the averages above in graphic form:

```
103        X
102
101
100
99                 X
98
97
96 ---------previous baseline score----------
95     X
94
93  X
92                     X  X  X  X  X
91             X
90
July 2014--------------------------------> June 2015
```

The takeaway points from this number crunch are:

1. I have improved four strokes from my previous baseline.
2. I occasionally, but not consistently, can break 90.
3. If I have a few bad rounds, I should not overreact. Things will even out.

4. Despite my improvement, I am still the worst golfer in my group.
5. The future is promising but uncertain. Continued improvement is not guaranteed.
6. Jonathan is a much better teacher than I am a student.
7. Numbers do not lie, but sometimes they don't tell the whole truth. I am a much better golfer now than a year ago, better than my scoring indicates.
8. If scoring is an art, I am a stick-figure golfer.
9. I'm glad that I decided to eliminate the no-golf option before this week. If not, my decision would have been a hard one.
10. Although I have improved only four strokes from my previous baseline, my scoring is at least ten strokes better than during last year's June slump and over thirty strokes better than the Shoal Creek Massacre of June 2014.

Reflecting on these take-home points, I consider my email to Jonathan one year ago a very wise decision. Over the past twelve months, he has done much more than improve my swing and my score. He has saved my game altogether, ended my thoughts of retirement, and made golf fun again.

So where do I go from here, now that my year of lessons is over? My goal of below-bogey scoring still remains the same, so I will continue my inexhaustible quest for 80s golf. With such unfinished business ahead, my chances of succeeding are much greater if I follow that wonderful piece of advice Jonathan gave at my last lesson in May. This nugget of truth, which I have kept secret until now, could be the answer to my prayers.

About halfway into that lesson, as I shared with him my scoring woes, Jonathan turned toward me and said, "Quit obsessing over the score! Obsess over your next shot!" In other words, the better fixation is the shot at hand, not the number on the scorecard. It was something he had said previously in other terms, but the way he phrased it on this day pierced my soul. To a golfer hopelessly obsessed with scoring, it was the Emancipation Proclamation of Golf. I know it seems absurd that one casual remark could have such an impact, but I swear on a stack of Bibles that it is true. The moment he said this, I was miraculously set free from numerical bondage. It was nothing less than an inner paradigm shift.

The same advice was echoed last week by my playing partner. Chris, a fellow resident of Cherokee Ridge, makes his living coaching volleyball but spends most of his free time playing golf and playing it well. He often shoots in the 70s, hits the ball a country mile, and has a good short game to match. He graciously asked me to play along with him and his precocious young daughter, Ellie. She is very good for her age and will get better and better over time.

Thirteen holes into the round, I was one-under bogey golf. I knew that a bogey on each of the remaining five holes would yield an 89 on my scorecard. I was confident and optimistic. My high hopes, however, were crushed when I promptly carded a 9 on the par-five fourteenth. From that point on, my chance of breaking 90 gone, I lost all confidence and willpower and finished the last four holes with a bogey, triple bogey, bogey, and double bogey, for a disappointing back-nine score of 51.

As we walked the course that day, the bits and pieces of advice Chris gave me were carbon copies of Jonathan's: (1) "Be confident and positive to the point of delusion." (2) "Assume an alter ego on the course, one that will never give up or lose focus." (3) "Randy Stewart is a better golfer than he thinks he is." (4) "Concentrate only on your next shot. Remember: golf should be played at the speed of smell."

In only a few holes, Chris diagnosed me all too well. I have a tendency to fret over past mistakes and to fear future ones. I am also inclined to obsess over my score at the end of the round, not on the shot at hand. For me, failure to break 90 equals total failure. But according to Jonathan and Chris, this should not be the case. Not concentrating completely on the next shot is failure, nothing else. To score better, my focus must change from the score itself to the shot at hand.

My future rounds of golf at Cherokee Ridge will be dedicated to this approach. Although I will continue to keep score, my single focus will be the shot before me. I will try to remain positive and confident to the point of delusion. I will even assume a golfing alter ego on the course to help me succeed.

After much thought, I have decided to assume the personality of Wile E. Coyote during my golfing rounds. He has all the qualities a would-be bogey golfer needs. He is always looking for a birdie. He never quits trying, despite his past failures. He lives in the present, focusing entirely on his next attempt to achieve his goal. Even though he is hopelessly behind on the scoreboard, he continues as if nothing bad has ever happened. He seems obsessed with the task at hand and oblivious to the score. In short, he is the poster child for delusional positivity.

Chapter 28: Settling the Score

One year ago I gave myself an ultimatum: "Improve at golf or quit!" I developed a plan and put it into action. First, I recruited Jonathan as my teacher. Next, I dedicated time to practicing on the range and playing on the course, and I did so in spite of cold weather, blustery winds, and drizzling rain. I became a student of the game, scanning the internet for golf tips and reading books about the technical and psychological fundamentals of the game. I kept statistics during my rounds, and I also followed my progress by keeping a diary of my journey.

Along the way, some of the things I learned about golf have surprised me. I discovered that...

... the golf swing is much harder to master than I anticipated.

... improving my golf swing does not necessarily guarantee an improved score.

... the mental aspect of golf is even more challenging than the technical.

... a very small change in a golf swing can make a huge difference in results, good or bad.

... trying to improve in golf can be more frustrating than playing carefree and can make golf less enjoyable.

... the success of a golf teacher, no matter how gifted he or she may be, is function of the student's potential. In other words, a teacher cannot work miracles.

... learning the correct way to swing makes golf more tolerable. Now, at least, I know what I am doing wrong.

... it will take longer than twelve months to right the wrongs of forty years. My journey toward improvement in golf has just begun.

... it is possible for a pitching wedge to control a golfer, not vice versa.

... the two most wonderful aspects of golf are its challenge and comradeship. I probably overemphasized the former this year and underestimated the latter. I need to restore balance soon.

Overall, the results of my journey have been positive. I now have a grasp of golf's fundamentals. I have a reproducible swing each day instead of a reactive swing-of-the-day. In fact, every part of my game is better than one year ago. The only negative is that scoring is the least improved aspect, and this is what I wanted to improve the most.

Seeking to learn the art of scoring, I paradoxically made a conscious effort this month not to keep score as much. Instead, I devoted these rounds to analyzing and correcting my poor swings. If I hit a bad shot, I hit it again with a different club or swing thought. In so doing, I hoped to learn why my shots go awry. In the midst of all this tinkering on the course, I did keep score on four days. My results fluctuated more than usual, from a low of 89 to a high of 102. The average was in the mid-90s. On an encouraging note, my final round of the month was the 89, hopefully a harbinger of things to come.

It is now time to find out where my golf game stands after one year of lessons and learning. I have decided to play several rounds over the next two months to determine my current golf handicap. Regardless of the outcome, I will then put the year behind me and move on. I am calling this series the Rider Cup, because my wife will ride with me during each round to verify my score. If Cathy is not an eyewitness, the round will not count.

In addition to the wife-in-the-cart rule, this is the format of the Rider Cup:

1. I will play a total of twelve rounds of golf from the blue tees at Cherokee Ridge (6385 yards).

2. I will use the USGA guidelines for obtaining a handicap: playing the ball as it lies but recording no more than a seven on any hole.

3. At the end of the twelfth round, I will compute my handicap. This is how I will grade my success:

HANDICAP	GRADE
> 21	F
19-21	D
16-18	C
13-15	B
10-12	A
< 10	A+

The professional Ryder Cup, held every two years, pits the best players in Europe against the best in America. In contrast, the Rider Cup at Cherokee Ridge will be held only this year and has only one competitor (yours truly). It pits the good golfer inside me against the bad golfer within.

Let the competition begin!

Chapter 29: A Handicapped Golfer

The rounds have been played. The scores have been posted. My handicap has been calculated, and the final grade in my journey toward golfing excellence has been recorded. Now that the last putt of the twelfth round has dropped into the cup, the results can be made public. They have been tabulated and certified by the distinguished accounting firm of Shank, Duckhook, and Bogey. Each score can also be verified by my wife, Cathy, who was the designated rider and eyewitness along the way. Despite what that golf pro insinuated after my first hole-in-one, her testimony can be trusted.

I will give you a round-by-round summary of my Rider Cup experience. After this, I will reveal to you my new official handicap index and the final grade on my journey. In review, every round was played from the blue tees at Cherokee Ridge (6385 yards, 70.6 Course Rating, 129 Slope). Using the USGA's recommendations for my level of play, seven was the maximum number I recorded on any hole. This is supposed to prevent occasional "come apart" holes from skewing one's handicap higher than it should be. In my experience, it also keeps one from quitting in mid-round and going back home.

Here is the Rider Cup statistical summary, plus a few explanatory notes:

ROUND #1 - August 13

The Good:	7 pars; 28 putts
The Okay:	5 bogeys; 4 of 14 up-and-downs
The Bad:	5 double bogeys
The Ugly:	only 2 GIR; 1 penguin (+4)

THE SCORE: 44 + 47= 91

ROUND #2 - August 18

The Good:	5 of 12 up-and-downs; 4 pars
The Okay:	32 putts; 9 bogeys
The Bad:	only 3 GIR; 4 double bogeys
The Ugly:	1 triple bogey

THE SCORE: 44 + 48 = 92

ROUND #3 - August 22

The Good:	5 pars, all on the back nine; 42 on the back nine
The Okay:	7 bogeys
The Bad:	6 double bogeys; only 4 GIR
The Ugly:	0 of 6 up-and-downs and 19 putts on the front nine

THE SCORE: 49 + 42 = 91

ROUND #4 - August 24

The Good:	4 pars and 1 birdie
The Okay:	7 bogeys, 32 putts
The Bad:	4 double bogeys
The Ugly:	2 triple bogeys; only 2 GIR; 2 of 15 up-and-downs

THE SCORE: 48 + 44 = 92

[Note: After four rounds, it seems I am programmed to shoot 91 or 92. I am averaging 46.25 on the front nine and 45.25 on the back nine. My weakness thus far is obvious: too few greens in regulation (2.75 per round) and too few successful up-and-downs from less than fifty yards (25%). To dip into the 80s, I must increase my GIR percentage or the number of up-and-downs per round. Of course, it would be best if I increased both.]

ROUND #5 - August 27

The Good: 4 pars and 1 birdie;
no triple bogeys

The Okay: 10 bogeys; 5 GIR;
15 putts on the back nine

The Bad: 3 double bogeys

The Ugly: 20 putts on the front nine;
2 of 13 up-and-downs

THE SCORE: 46 + 41 = 87

[Note: This was my lowest round at Cherokee Ridge since October of last year. The principal reason was the absence of a triple bogey or worse on my scorecard. The rare birdie also helped a lot.]

ROUND #6 - September 1

The Good: not a lot to brag about

The Okay: 4 pars and 7 bogeys

The Bad: 35 putts; only 4 GIR

The Ugly: 1 of 9 up-and-downs; 6 double
bogeys; 1 triple bogey

THE SCORE: 48 + 46 = 94

ROUND #7 - September 2

The Good: 5 of 13 up-and-downs; 5 pars

The Okay: 34 putts; 8 bogeys

The Bad: driver was erratic today;
2 double bogeys

The Ugly: failed to get out of two sand traps on first try; 3 triple bogeys

THE SCORE: 47 + 44 = 91

ROUND #8 - September 5

The Good: 5 pars; no three-putts; no triple bogeys

The Okay: 9 bogeys; 33 putts

The Bad: 4 double bogeys

The Ugly: 2 of 10 up-and-downs

THE SCORE: 45 + 44 = 89

ROUND #9 - September 10

The Good: 5 pars

The Okay: 7 bogeys; 34 putts (on bumpy, freshly aerated greens)

The Bad: 4 double bogeys; only 4 GIR; 3 of 11 up-and-downs; 2 three-putts

The Ugly: 2 triple bogeys; 4 bad bounces (e.g. directly behind trees)

THE SCORE: 45 + 48 = 93

ROUND #10 - September 13

The Good: 4 pars and 1 birdie (I sank a 50-footer); no lost balls (a rare feat)

The Okay: 10 bogeys; on or near the green in regulation on 14 holes; 33 putts

The Bad: only 3 GIR; 2 double bogeys (but no triple bogeys)

The Ugly: 3 of 15 up-and-downs

THE SCORE: 45 + 42 = 87

[Note: Between rounds 10 and 11 at Cherokee Ridge, I played eighteen holes with my friend Barry at Chesley Oaks. We played the ball down and putted everything out, stricter rules than we usually follow on this course. It turned out to be a day to remember. After a rather lackluster 46 on the front nine, yours truly carded an impressive 36 on the back. It was as if all the golfing demons that usually torment me decided to take a siesta for nine holes. I was on the green in regulation on five holes and got up and down successfully on three of my four opportunities. The result was one birdie, seven pars, and one bogey. My 36 and 82, respectively, were the lowest nine-hole and eighteen-hole scores of my life. Granted, it was accomplished on an easy venue, but no one can play par golf anywhere for that many holes unless he hits a lot of good shots. While I do not expect this to be the norm from now on—indeed, it may never be repeated—it is extremely satisfying that I did it at least once.]

ROUND #11 - October 13

The Good:	29 putts; 2 birdies; 3 pars
The Okay:	8 bogeys
The Bad:	only 2 of 9 up-and-downs; only 4 GIR
The Ugly:	one triple bogey

THE SCORE: 46 + 43 = 89

[Note: This sub-90 round was played exactly one month after my last round at Cherokee Ridge and just four days after returning from a week in Guatemala. I consider it an encouraging sign that I can shoot less than bogey golf after such a layoff. Does this mean that my new swing is now my permanent swing, the only one my mind and muscles remember? I sincerely hope so.]

ROUND #12 - October 15
    The Good: 4 of 10 successful up-and-downs
    The Okay: 3 pars and 9 bogeys;
                     no triple bogeys
    The Bad: 6 double bogeys; poor ball striking
                     (only 2 GIR and 7 near-GIR)
    The Ugly: one four-putt (after reaching the
                     green in regulation)
    THE SCORE: 48 + 45 = 93

[The results of my last round should put to rest any thought that I have embellished the events in this book. It would have been great to have ended my Rider Cup experience with the round of my life or a hole-out from the fairway on the final hole. Despite my efforts, this did not happen. My round today was very pedestrian, even below average. The good news is that I played badly and shot 93. Before I started my quest toward improvement, I would have considered this one of my best rounds. Perhaps this is an appropriate way for a bogey golfer's diary to end: describing how "not bad" he is instead of how "good" is. I'm like the ugliest girl in class who brags, after several trips to the dentist, that only half her teeth are decayed. My game is not pretty, by any means, but it has improved enough to make me smile, in spite of all the negatives that remain.]

Here is a summary of the twelve rounds above:

    lowest score: 87
    highest score: 94

average score: 90.8
average # of GIR: 3.4
average # of near-GIR (<50 yards): 7.8
% up-and-downs (from <50 yards): 25.7%
average # of putts: 32.8
average # of birdies: 0.5
average # of pars: 4.4
average # of bogeys: 8.0
average # of double bogeys: 4.3
average # of triple bogeys or higher: 0.83

****

Before I reveal to you my golf handicap, let me give a few basics about the USGA's handicap system: how a handicap is calculated and what it does and does not indicate.

What is the purpose of a handicap?

The handicap system serves to level the playing field, allowing a bogey golfer like me to compete with a good golfer like Jonathan. Better players have lower handicaps. The worse you are, the higher your handicap will be. If Jonathan and I squared off in a match, we could subtract our handicaps from our eighteen-hole scores to yield an adjusted score for that day. The golfer with the lowest adjusted score would be the winner. Therefore, thanks to the handicap system, golfers of unequal ability can play in the same foursome, give their best efforts, and still enjoy a competitive round. No other sport provides a way for the best to play against the worst.

How is the handicap calculated?

The formula for establishing a golf handicap is rather complex. It seems like something Albert Einstein would have rattled off on his deathbed while delirious. To convert my twelve rounds into a handicap, I had to know three things:

1. my four lowest Adjusted Gross Scores (87, 87, 89, 89; average = 88)
2. the USGA Course Rating for Cherokee Ridge from the blue tees (70.6), which is the average score a par golfer would be expected to shoot
3. the USGA Slope Rating for Cherokee Ridge from the blue tees (129), which indicates how difficult the course is to a bogey golfer

Knowing these numbers, I entered them into the following formula to discover my handicap index:

Step 1
I subtracted the USGA Course Rating (70.6) from my average Adjusted Gross Score (88).

$$88 - 70.6 = 17.4$$

Step 2
I multiplied the answer in Step 1 by 113 (the slope of a course of average difficulty).

$$17.4 \times 113 = 1966.2$$

Step 3
I divided the answer in Step 2 by 129 (the USGA Slope Rating from the blue tees at Cherokee Ridge).

$$1966.2 \text{ divided by } 129 = 15.24$$

Step 4

I multiplied the answer in Step 3 by 0.96 and then dropped any number to the right of the tenths.

$$15.24 \times 0.96 = 14.63 = 14.6$$

14.6 is my handicap index. Game on, Jonathan!

What does my handicap tell me?

Since my handicap index is derived from my lowest adjusted scores, it is not a measure of my average scoring ability. Instead, it is more indicative of my scoring potential. What my handicap index tells me, then, is that I have the potential to frequently shoot 86-87 on a par-72 layout of average difficulty.

Cherokee Ridge from the blue tees, however, is not average in difficulty. Its slope rating of 129, well above the average of 113, testifies to its severity. This is one of the reasons breaking 90 from the blues has been so challenging here. By playing an easier course, such as Chesley Oaks (slope 106) or by "playing it forward" from the white tees at Cherokee Ridge (slope 118), scoring in the 80s should become the rule, not the exception.

This is exactly what I plan to do. Now that my yearlong journey is over, I will no longer consider it necessary to tee it up from the blues at the Ridge. I will choose to play from a variety of tees on a variety of courses, hopefully bringing the word "fun" back into golf.

To be honest, I am quite relieved that this odyssey has ended. When improvement is the only goal, frustration and disillusionment can begin to rule the day. Now that my lessons are over and my handicap has been determined, I can once again focus on the positives of golf not tied to the final score: the joy of being with friends, the breathtaking beauty of God's creation, and the thrill of a great shot (even in the middle of a poor round). I will, like every avid golfer, continue my quest for improvement, but I will have a more balanced perspective as I move ahead. I still want to get better, but getting better is not all I want.

What is my final grade?

I gave you my grading system for the Rider Cup in the previous chapter. The final grade on my report card, therefore, based on my 14.6 handicap index, is a B. On the negative side, this could stand for *bogey golf*, which continues to be my goal at the start of a round and my average score at its end. But looking at it positively, it could stand for *better golf*, which accurately describes the status of my game.

When I think back to the golfer I was at the Shoal Creek Massacre and compare him to the golfer of the Rider Cup, the distance I have traveled comes into focus. I play the game much better now, and I understand the game better, too. I am still not the golfer I should be and am hopefully not the golfer I shall be. But this one thing is sure: thanks in large part to Jonathan, I am not the golfer I used to be.

Chapter 30: Reward and Punishment

I played Shoal Creek again today.

Yes, I garnered the courage to tackle the course that brought me to the brink of golfing despair last year. I took Jonathan along with me this time, not as my teacher but as a member of my foursome. I considered a round at Shoal Creek a fitting "thank you" for all he has done for me. He told me a while back that he had played the course once several years ago and had longed for an opportunity to play it again.

In addition to being an end-of-the-journey gift to Jonathan, the round today at Shoal Creek seemed like a perfect way to end my narrative. I wrote the first chapter of this book immediately after playing here. I am likewise completing its final chapter after playing here. The two rounds at Shoal Creek, therefore, serve as bookends that neatly bracket the body of this story.

There was a third reason I decided to return to Shoal Creek, a therapeutic one. Psychologists often encourage traumatized patients to revisit places where terrible events have occurred. By doing so, they are able to loosen the trauma's grip on their lives. In the same way, I considered going back to Shoal Creek a chance to further silence the golfing demons that have tormented me for years. In June of 2014, they used Shoal Creek to humiliate me. I wanted to confront them again at the same location and walk away the victor instead of the victim.

Of course, the round today was also another way to gauge the status of my golf game. Establishing a handicap had given me a sense of where my game is at the present. Comparing today with my three previous rounds at Shoal Creek would show me how much I have improved from the past. In particular, I was eager to contrast today's performance with the Shoal Creek Massacre. Would my experience be different this time? Would I score better? Would I think clearer? Would I leave the course happier than I did that dreadful day?

The answer to all the questions above is, "Yes!" The experience was different, the score better, the thoughts clearer, and the countenance happier as I walked off the course. Granted, there were several negatives about the round, but these were over-shadowed by the positives. Viewing golf from the perspective of reward and punishment, today was a win for the reward side of the ledger.

On the punishment side is the following list:

1. **a total gross score of 106 (48-58) and an adjusted gross score of 100 (48-52)**, well above bogey golf and six strokes worse than my highest adjusted gross score during the Rider Cup. A triple bogey and two penguins on the back nine were my undoing.
2. **poor pitching and chipping**, which explains much of the higher scoring today.
3. **too many bunkers hit and not enough good bunker shots**, which explains the rest of the higher scoring.
4. **too many putts**, although the speed of the greens was responsible to some degree.

On the reward side, the list is considerably longer:

1. **an A+ driver** – I hit my driver a total of fifteen times. I hit it well fourteen times. And I hit it longer than ever before.
2. **a positive mental outlook** – Even when shots went awry, I remained upbeat and forward-looking.
3. **a miracle worker** – I am usually relegated to being a witness of the miraculous on a golf course. Today I was the beneficiary and my partners the observers. On one hole, my ball was headed out of bounds to the right but bounced off a tree to within six feet of the green. Even more incredible was my hole-out later in the round. I watched my yellow ball squirt between two trees, sail over a bunker, bounce once on the green, and dive straight into the hole. I doubt I could repeat the result in a thousand more tries.
4. **the up-and-down of the day** – On the par-three eighth hole, I was four feet off the green to the right with a bunker directly between me and the flag. At the urging of my caddy, I took an aggressive line, skirted the edge of the bunker, and rolled the ball to within six feet of the cup. I then sank the downhiller for an unexpected par.
5. **complimentary partners** – All members of my foursome praised how I hit my full clubs, especially my driver. Both Craig and Larry, who were eyewitnesses to the Massacre at Shoal Creek, seemed impressed with the progress I had made between then and now.
6. **fellowship with friends** – The entire round was sprinkled with laughter, small talk, courtesy,

encouragement, and mutual admiration. This wonderful mix continued during a late lunch at the clubhouse and on our ride home to Marshall County. After a year of playing alone, I enjoyed the comradery of playing partners more than ever before.

7. **God's nature at its best** – We experienced Shoal Creek at its finest: bright sun, a gentle breeze, comfortable temperatures, autumn colors, and abundant greenery. I found myself absorbed in the beauty of the course.

8. **no massacre today** – My score of 106, though not as good as I had hoped, was about twenty strokes better than June of 2014. The round had its ugly moments, but in no way was it reminiscent of the bloodbath I endured during the Shoal Creek Massacre.

9. **a top-rate caddy** – He spends many weeks on the Web.com Tour carrying the bag of his nephew, so he is accustomed to much better play. But he treated me as if I were playing in the final pairing of The Masters. He gave advice but was not overbearing. He helped me know when to avoid risks and when to be more aggressive. It was at his prodding that I attempted and executed that difficult up-and-down on the par-three eighth.

10. **no last place trophy today** – Each of us kept our own score, so I don't know what my three partners shot. I do know that none of us played to his potential, each scoring at least ten strokes above expectations. Although I did not shoot lower than Jonathan or Craig, I was competitive from hole to hole. I was third in total score overall, and I won two holes outright. During the

Shoal Creek Massacre, in contrast, I was a distant fourth in my foursome and did not win a single hole.

****

Located between the sixth tee and the seventh green of Cherokee Ridge, my home course, is an old Indian cemetery. It consists of about thirty flat rocks that serve as the headstones. This ancient burial site was discovered in 1991 when the course was being built and was left intact out of respect for the dead. Obviously, these Indians had no idea that their bodies would someday rest on a golf course. I have often wondered what they would say if they could revisit their stomping ground today.

Unlike those Cherokees, some people have actually chosen a golf course as their place of burial. At Chesley Oaks, our FedUp Cup venue, a tombstone can be seen to the left of the cart path as a player moves from the second green to the third tee. In my opinion, being buried on a golf course is not a great idea, but it is an especially bad one if the grave is located along a cart path just beyond a green. Golfers tend to curse and complain a lot as they walk off greens toward the next tee. Why would anyone choose to rest forever at a place like this, where brute honesty and profanity abound? By the way, if you want to know the true measure of a man, listen to what he says immediately after ending a phone call or finishing a golf hole.

Even stranger to me are those who wish to have their ashes scattered over a golf course. I personally prefer entombment to cremation. Even if I change my mind, I sure won't choose a golf course as the depository of my charred remains. For one thing, it would signify that my priorities in life were out of order. Why not choose instead my home, my church, or my clinic in Guatemala? What's more, I am afraid of what would happen if my ashes were dumped from an airplane onto Cherokee Ridge. I fear they would react symbolically. Regardless of the direction the wind is blowing, some would travel right, some left, some short, and some long. None, I am convinced, would land on a green.

I know of several people who have died during a round of golf. In my ER years, I treated a few men who suffered a cardiac arrest on the course. None survived, because it usually takes too long for help to arrive to resuscitate a golfer. Harlice Keown, one of my father's dearest friends, died this way a few years back. I was told that he was lining up a birdie putt when he collapsed. If being on the green in regulation is a prerequisite for dying on a golf course, I am safer there than any place I can imagine.

When all is said is done, I have no desire to die on a golf course, be buried on a golf course, or be scattered over a golf course. But I do have one burning desire about golf, a yearning that is stronger today than ever before. Above bogey or below, I want to enjoy this fascinating game as long as I live.

AFTERWORD

Dear Reader,

Golf, people often say, tends to mirror life. It is just as true, however, that life frequently transcends golf. During Randy's weeks in Guatemala, for instance, the enormity of the need completely removes golf from his mind. No one can walk through the garbage dump these people call home and watch them scavenge for their shelter and sustenance without being overwhelmed. At that moment, reality trumps recreation.

Jonathan has likewise visited a part of the world where golf becomes meaningless. His annual mission trips to Romania are life-altering experiences. When he returns home, a piece of his heart and soul remains there. In a spiritual sense, he considers the Romanians lifelong playing partners. They walk together down a fairway sown with the Word of God, nourished by the Water of Life, and sustained by the Light of the World.

Before you close this book and place it on a shelf or in a drawer, we want to ask you also to partner with us. There are several ways you can do so:

1. Purchase more copies of this book. (The proceeds will be split evenly between our Guatemalan and Romanian ministries.)

2. Donate money to our organizations.

3. Pray for these dear people in Central America and Europe and for us as we seek to minister to them.

It doesn't matter if you purchase one copy, donate one dollar, or pray one minute. God can multiply your gift for His glory. In the New Testament, a boy's meager lunch became a crowd's buffet. If you share what's in your hand at this moment, a similar miracle just might happen. In mission work, as in the golf swing, little things can make a world of difference.

Randy Stewart and Jonathan Lynch

To order more copies of this book

www.amazon.com

www.completelynovel.com

**To learn more about the
Guatemalan and Romanian ministries**

www.fourfriendsinternational.blogspot.com

www.madisonassociation.org/romania-partnership

To give to the Guatemalan ministry, send to:

FOUR FRIENDS INTERNATIONAL

C/O THE BAPTIST FOUNDATION OF ALABAMA

7650 HALCYON SUMMIT DRIVE

MONTGOMERY, AL 36117

To give to the Romanian ministry, send to:

SIBIU, ROMANIA MISSIONS PARTNERSHIP

C/O MADISON BAPTIST ASSOCIATION

2318 WHITESBURG DRIVE SOUTH

HUNTSVILLE, AL 35801

To contact Jonathan Lynch or Randy Stewart

jlynch6783@gmail.com ❖ randystewartmd@yahoo.com

Other books by **Randall Stewart**

5 Reasons: Why I Still Believe in God

Dear God, You Sure Don't Act like You're Alive

If God Is "I AM", then Who Am I?

Before the Trumpet Sounds:
When Jesus Came to the Tennessee River Valley

The Word Made Fresh: 1000 Bible Questions

Once Upon a Holy Night:
a collection of Christmas stories

purchase at amazon.com or completelynovel.com